Serbian Fol

Fairy tales and

Maximilian A. Mügge

Alpha Editions

This edition published in 2020

ISBN : 9789354016943

Design and Setting By
Alpha Editions
email - alphaedis@gmail.com

As per information held with us this book is in Public Domain.
This book is a reproduction of an important historical work. Alpha Editions uses the best technology to reproduce historical work in the same manner it was first published to preserve its original nature. Any marks or number seen are left intentionally to preserve its true form.

Serbian Folk Songs
Fairy Tales and Proverbs

BY

MAXIMILIAN A. MÜGGE

Author of " Friedrich Nietzsche : His Life and Work;"
" Eugenics and the Superman;" " Heinrich von Treitschke,"
&c,

London:
DRANE'S
DANEGELD HOUSE
82a FARRINGDON STREET, E.C.

To
Miss LAURA P. DURBAN

"ἄνδρα δ' ὠφελεῖν ἀφ' ὧν
ἔχοι τε καὶ δύναιτο κάλλιστος πόνων."

SOPHOCLES

PREFACE

In spite of an ever-growing network of tight-fitting iron ribbons and copper threads, our old planet Earth still refuses to be squeezed and reduced to a nicely manageable globe, just so many times the size of the Albert Hall, with properly numbered and defined departments, with a common larder and with—an American Board of Directors. Distance and language are yet barriers proving as formidable to " progress " as racial antagonism, human inertia, greed, and ambition.

True, only about thirty-six hours are needed nowadays to travel from London to Serbia. No longer does the traveller settle all his worldly affairs before he crosses the frontier at Belgrade, as the author of *Eothen* did in 1835. But that the relatively shorter distance has not achieved everything Miss Mary E. Durham has shown us in her delightful book, *Through the Lands of the Serb*. It is but a little over ten years since she drew her charming word-pictures of impressions during her journey; but we read, " Guards and ticket-collectors agreed in telling me that it was impossible for me to go to Belgrade." When she travelled from Niš to Pirot an officious and stupid fellow-traveller actually succeeded in frightening her about her dangerous enterprise, " until I had a hail-Cæsar-we-who-are-to-die-salute-thee feeling, which became less and less dignified as the West Balkans themselves came into sight. We reached Pirot, and I descended from the train in a state not unlike ' funk.' "

PREFACE

During the last eighteen months Serbia has come nearer to us. Fighting against terrible odds, our brave little ally held up the " walk-over " of her powerful northern neighbour, and thrice she threw back the vast armies of Austria. Little Serbia not only impaired the prestige of her foe, but also kept fully occupied those legions of Austria which otherwise would have been employed elsewhere. The fine peasant army of Serbia was the rampart which for long weary months defied the Central Powers in their policy of joining up with the Turk.

Finally, however, gallant little Serbia went down under the avalanches from North and East.

She had done all she could. Yet her heroic army still exists to fight again for Liberty and National Unity. The Spirit of the Serb is unbroken. And the Great Powers amongst the Allies will never forget their debt to Serbia. I cannot state the case better than by quoting Professor R. W. Seton-Watson :—" She has borne the burden and heat of the day, she has rendered signal services to the allied cause, and her valour has finally dispersed the calumnies with which her enemies so long assailed her reputation. . . . I have no hesitation in asking you to sympathise with Serbia !"

The object of this book is to enlist such sympathy. England was the champion of Greece and Italy when these two countries fought for their liberty and unity. And Serbia, who, within a hundred years after her liberation from four centuries of Turkish " rule," has performed the miracle of almost attaining the civilisation of Western

PREFACE

Europe, deserves likewise the championship of the free Britons.

The folk-songs given in this volume are for the greater part taken from J. Bowring's *Serbian Popular Poetry*, O. Meredith's (Bulwer-Lytton) *The National Songs of Serbia*, and from various reviews, and some I have translated from the Serbian original. I have made some alterations in those poems which are reprinted. The fairy-tales and proverbs I have translated from Miss Karadžić's *Volksmärchen der Serben*. The music given in the appendix has been taken from F. S. Kuhać, *Južno-Slavjenske Narodne Popievke*.

I am under great obligation to Professor Bogdan Popović and to Professor Pavle Popović, both of Belgrade University, for the kind help they have given me; and a subsidy granted by the Serbian Government to the publisher may also be most gratefully acknowledged.

I am personally indebted to the present Earl of Lytton for the kind permission to make extracts from his father's book, and to the Rev. Edgar Francis Bowring, Rector of Farncombe, for kindly allowing me to make use of Sir John Bowring's book.

Thanks are due to the officials of the Reading Room of the British Museum and to Frank Compton Price, Esquire, who have assisted me in the endeavour to trace *Translations from the Serbian Minstrelsy*, a book privately printed, reviewed without the author's name being given in *The Quarterly Review*, 1826, and mentioned in *Chambers's Edinburgh Journal*, 1845. We did not succeed.   Perhaps some reader of this anthology may be more fortunate.

M. A. M.,
Royal Sussex Regiment.

Fort Hill Camp, Newhaven,
    April, 1916.

CONTENTS

PREFACE	5
SERBO-CROAT ORTHOGRAPHY	13
INTRODUCTION	17

FOLK SONGS. (The Roman figures in brackets refer to the volume, the Arabic figures in brackets to the number of the poem in that volume, of V. S. Karadžić, *Srpske Narodne Pjesme*, Beograd, 1891-1902.) ... 43

CEASE THY WARBLINGS, NIGHTINGALE! (I., 566)	45
THE MAIDEN AND THE VIOLET. (I., 322)	45
SOLICITUDE. (I., 524)	46
SPRING SONG. (I., 546)	46
THE ABSENT LOVER. (I., 318)	47
THE MAIDEN AND THE TALISMAN. (I., 498)	47
CARES AND CURSES. (I., 360)	48
LONGINGS. (I., 350)	48
THE UNHAPPY BRIDE. (I., 609)	49
REMEMBRANCE. (I., 551)	49
FROZEN HEART. (I., 311)	50
DESPAIR. (I., 581)	50

CONTENTS

FOLK SONGS (*continued*)—

RETALIATION. (I., 351)	51
THE PALE HAG JEALOUSY. (I., 359)	52
LOVE AND SLEEP. (I., 455)	52
THE MAIDEN'S APPEAL. (I., 310)	54
THE LOVER'S BLESSING. (I., 362)	54
LOVE AND DIGNITY. (I., 526)	55
SURRENDER. (I., 594)	55
THE HUNTER'S PRIZE. (I., 432)	57
REMINISCENCE. (I., 564)	57
KEEPSAKES. (I., 555)	58
MERRIMENT. (I., 487)	59
LOVE'S TRIAL. (I., 738)	59
THE KNITTER. (I., 397)	61
MAY AND DECEMBER. (I., 401)	61
ALL'S WELL THAT ENDS WELL. (I., 705)	62
THE ROGUISH MAIDEN. (I., 253)	63
HASANAGINICA. (III., 513)	64
HAJKUNA'S MARRIAGE. (III., 83)	68
THE DEATH OF IVO. (III., 51)	72
JAKSIC DMITAR AND JAKSIC BOGDANA. (II., 97)	75
MARKO'S FALCON. (II., 69)	78

CONTENTS 11

FOLK SONGS (*continued*)—

MARKO AND THE MOORISH MAIDEN. (II., 63) ...	82
THE DEATH OF MARKO. (II., 73) ...	85
THE FALL OF THE SERBIAN EMPIRE. (II., 45) ...	90
KOSOVO. (II., 44; Lines 119-204) ...	93

FAIRY TALES. (The figures given in brackets refer to the numbers of the fairy tales in V. S. Karadžić, *Srpske Narodne Pripovijetke*, 1870 and 1853 editions.) ... 99

WHY THE SOLE OF MAN'S FOOT IS FLAT....(18) ...	101
THE RAM WITH THE GOLDEN FLEECE. (12) ...	102
ABOUT THE MAIDEN SWIFTER THAN A HORSE. (24) ...	111
HONESTY IS NE'ER AN ILL PENNYWORTH. (7) ...	113
THE CASTLE IN CLOUDLAND. (2) ...	116
THE WONDERFUL HAIR. (31) ...	121
CLOTHES MADE OF DEW AND SUNRAYS. (23) ...	125
FATE. (13) ...	129
SOLOMON CURSED BY HIS MOTHER. (31) ...	139
THE TRIUMPH OF JUSTICE. (16) ...	142

PROVERBS ...	147
BIBLIOGRAPHY ...	155
APPENDIX: SERBIAN TEXTS AND MELODIES ...	162

SERBO-CROAT ORTHOGRAPHY

(From *Southern Slav Culture*, published by the Jugoslav Committee in London.)

š = sh in " ship."
č = ch in " church."
ć = ditto (softer).
c = ts in " cats."
ž = j in " jour."
j = y in " your."

INTRODUCTION

INTRODUCTION

POLITICAL IMPORTANCE OF SERBIAN FOLK-SONGS

In his excellent book, *Hero-Tales and Legends of the Serbians*, Voislav M. Petrović tells us, " That a distinct Serbian Nation has survived the dark days of Turkish rule is due to the National Songs of Serbia."

These songs told of great deeds and men, of bygone splendour and of a glorious independence in the past. Theirs was the " immortal Voice, born of Golden Hope !"

Of course the national church, national customs like the national dance, the Kolo, contributed towards preserving and strengthening the spiritual bonds that held the Serbians together. But the national songs more than anything else ensured the continuance of the Serbian Language when Turkish was the official language of the Government and administration. They kept alive the spirit of nationality during those centuries of living death under the Crescent. The Christian nations under the Moslem's sway have been compared with the Sleeping Beauty. For a long time nothing could penetrate the strong and cruel thorns around the Castle of the Middle Ages, the Balkans. But the National Muse at last succeeded.

And the National Muse is not yet dead.

In 1833 Karadžić wrote :—" To-day it is in Bosnia, Hercegovina, Montenegro, and the mountainous regions of Serbia, where our people's love for the heroic poetry of the past is found to be strongest and most general. There is hardly a house anywhere in these districts, without a gouslé, and it would be difficult to come across a man who cannot play it."

We read in E. L. Mijatović's *Kosovo* :—" Even the present member of the National Assembly not infrequently speaks in blank verse when his feelings are roused to an exalted pitch. During the winter of 1873-74, happening to be in Kragujevac during the meeting of the National Assembly, I had the opportunity of hearing a certain peasant, Anta Neshich, member of the Assembly, recite in blank verse to numerous audiences outside the Assembly Room the whole debate on the bill for introducing the new monetary system into Serbia, concluding with the final acceptation of the bill."

During the battle of Prilip in November, 1912, the Serbian soldiers had been told not to attack the Turks before the proper order was given, but to wait until the effect of the Serbian artillery could be observed. In front of them on the mount of Prilip stood the Castle of Marko Kraljević. Suddenly the Serbian Infantry began to move, and rushed forward. The appeals of their General, the remonstrances of their officers, all proved futile. On they rushed. The commanding General expected defeat and disgrace. On they rushed. The Serbian artillery had to cease firing, or they would have killed their own comrades now crossing bayonets with the Turks. And a few minutes later—the Serbian national colours were fluttering on Marko's

INTRODUCTION 19

Castle. The Turks were beaten. When the perplexed General, although very much pleased, censured his soldiers on parade for their disobedience, he heard, " Marko Kraljević commanded us all the time, ' Forward.' Did you not see him on his Šarac?" " It was clear to me," the General said to some of his friends later on, " that the tradition of Marko Kraljević was so deeply engraved on the hearts of those honest and heroic men, that in their vivid enthusiasm they had seen the incarnation of their hero."

" Spes mihi prima Deus " is the inscription on Parlaghy's fine picture of King Peter. The Serbian nation may well take it as a motto in these days of darkness. Marko is not dead. Like another Barbarossa, he is but asleep within a mountain cavern. One day he will awaken and lead his Serbians to victory. Dušan's empire may yet be built up again and unite all the Southern Slavs, the Jugoslavs, under one sceptre.

If there is to be a future in spite of the faults of the past, if there is to be victory after defeat, nations, like individuals, need Henley's unconquerable soul. At present Serbia lies prostrate in the dust, crushed under the accumulated weight of failures and falsehoods. But she will not die. Eight centuries of national aspirations cannot be baulked by the shifting of boundaries on the map. There is a Serbian proverb which may be rendered, " Mightier than the will of the Kaiser is the will of God." Serbia's spirit, never yet broken, her unconquerable Soul, will still survive, and amongst her strongest and most faithful allies are her own children, the Serbian National Songs!

SPLENDOUR OF SERBIA IN THE PAST

" In no country in the world," we are assured by Mijatović, " are the illiterate and uneducated peasantry so conversant with their national history as in Serbia." That wonderful retentive memory which individuals of younger and unlettered nations so often possess enables many children of the soil to recite sometimes even thirty, fifty, or a hundred long poems. Owing to their tendency towards adapting themselves easily to the individual's fancy, and therefore undergoing constant change, such songs are not, scientifically speaking, historical documents; but the poems now at our disposal in the large State edition of Karadžić's collection are in their fixed form of the greatest historical interest, since they reflect in varying degrees of exactness the political, social, and ethical development of Serbia.

The Serbian language is spoken by about nine million people in Bosnia, Croatia, Dalmatia, Hercegovina, the Turkish vilayet of Kosovo, Western Macedonia, Montenegro, the sanjak of Novi-Bazar, the present kingdom of Serbia, Old Serbia, Slavonia, and in Southern Hungary.

Already in the fifth century of our era the Jugoslavs seem to have appeared on the Lower Danube. Soon they spread towards the South and the West. In order to wage war with the Persians, the East Roman emperor Herakleos (610-41) had to with-

INTRODUCTION 21

draw all his garrison troops from European Byzance, and the Jugoslavs occupied and settled in the Balkan territory affected. The Byzantine ruler graciously gave them permission to do so on condition that they acknowledged the supremacy of Byzantium. In 680, Tartar tribes, called Bulgars, arrived on the scene, conquered and subjected eight tribes of the new settlers, and from that time onwards until the present day Serbs and Bulgars have been enemies. The remaining tribes, however, gathered around the leading clans, the Hrvats (Croats) and the Serbs, slowly crystallizing into several small States. The designation "Serb" occurs for the first time in 822; the term "Croat" in 845. Cyril and Method, the two great Slav apostles, introduced Christianity to the Northern Slavs of Moravia and Pannonia; they translated the Bible and the first liturgic writings into the Old Slav tongue, and thus made Christianity accessible for the whole of the Slav race. Clement (916), one of their first disciples, introduced Christianity and the Slav liturgy among the Jugoslavs.

Gradually the several small States grew in strength; rivals amongst themselves, but usually unanimous against the hated Bulgars and Byzantines. Again and again attempts were made to shake off the suzerainty of East-Rome. Men like Chaslav Klonimirović and Samuel tried to establish a union of all the Jugoslav States. But internal dissensions and external foes shattered their schemes. Two more enemies arose; ambitious, greedy Venice in the West, and the vigorous, and flourishing young State of Hungary. The

Pope, with true Christian tolerance, urged the kings of Hungary to conquer the Serbian States, and either crush the heretics of the Serbian Church or bring them back to his fold.

In spite of her enemies, Serbia, however, became steadily stronger. Nemanja succeeded in establishing a union, and his son Stevan (1196-1228) proclaimed himself a king. From 1220 until 1346, when Dušan had himself proclaimed Tsar and founded the Serbian Empire, the rising State had seven kings, as once another favourite of Fortune.

In the beginning of the 14th century Bulgaria and Serbia were once again fighting one another. On the side of the Bulgarians were Byzantine armies. Byzantium, the modern Constantinople, was still the capital of the Eastern Roman Empire. And then, as to-day, the soldiers of Serbia were brave men. The Bulgarian army was utterly routed in 1330 at Velbouzd. The Serbian advance forces during that battle were led by the heir to the crown, Stevan Dušan, who distinguished himself greatly.

The year after the battle of Velbouzd he ascended the throne. The favourite of his people, twenty years of age, beloved by his charming and courageous wife Ielena, the young king might well have rested on the laurels he had gathered. But the spirit of Alexander the Great seemed to have found another re-incarnation.

Stevan's first act was to enter and occupy Macedonia. The Byzantine emperor, Andronicus, was in Salonika, and Stevan besieged him. But for the mischance of a threatening Hungarian invasion,

Stevan would probably have succeeded in overthrowing the tottering Eastern Empire there and then. As it was, he had to give up the siege and hasten northwards to meet the Hungarian invaders. They were beaten. Stevan followed up his victory, conquering Albania and seizing Epirus. Henceforth he styled himself King of the Serbs and Albanians.

In 1341 the emperor Andronicus III. died. With his death begins that period of anarchy which ended with the fall of the Eastern Roman Empire, with the victory of the Crescent over the Cross in Byzantium.

Andronicus left his throne to the child-emperor, John V. The child's regent, Kantakouzene, was an ambitious and unscrupulous scoundrel. Disagreeing with the Empress-Mother, he left Byzantium and proclaimed himself Emperor at Demotica.

Stevan Dušan at first sided with Kantakouzene, but, disgusted with the usurper's duplicity, joined forces with the Empress-Mother.

Then Kantakouzene committed the crime of crimes. He asked the Turks to come over to Europe and help him. Never before had they dared to set foot on European soil. Kantakouzene lifted the lid from Pandora's box, and to-day we are still suffering from the ills he brought upon Europe.

The fierce fanatics of the Crescent came. At first they were victorious, but the indomitable king of the Serbs was not going to be beaten. In 1345 Stevan conquered almost the whole of Macedonia and part of Thracia.

His was indeed a great realm; in addition to the lands inherited, he now ruled over Albania, Epirus, Macedonia, and Thracia; Bulgaria was practically a protectorate.

The Serbian Church, which, under Nemanja's son Sava, the Serbian St. Sabbes, had become autonomous, was raised to the dignity of a Patriarchate.

On the 16th April, 1346, at Skoplje (Uskub), the Serbian Patriarch, in the presence of the Bulgarian Patriarch, placed the Imperial crown upon Stevan's head. At the same time Stevan's young son was crowned a king.

There can be but little doubt that the Emperor of Serbia foresaw the impending doom of the enfeebled Eastern Roman Empire, and conceived the magnificent plan of building up a mighty empire on its ruins to be a bulwark against the Turks and the realization of the Serbian ideal of Balkan supremacy.

Within a few years he added to the Serbian Empire Acarnania, Belgrade, Bosnia, Etolia, the Hercegovina, and Thessaly.

Wisely, he did not neglect the internal affairs of his country. The Serbian National Assembly promulgated (1349) the "Zakonik," a law code, certainly one of the best amongst mediæval law books.

The wicked Kantakouzene meanwhile had been busy too. In 1352 he came with a powerful host, supported by his allies, the Turks, and Stevan and John V. were beaten, owing to the Bulgarians forsaking them at the last moment before the battle. Kantakouzene now held Byzantium.

INTRODUCTION 25

Within a few years Stevan, however, had recovered and returned to his Imperial policy. At the head of 80,000 veteran soldiers the undaunted Serbian Emperor set out for Byzantium. Victory was with him. Town after town surrendered. The foe retreated. Stevan was almost within sight of his goal, when suddenly, on the 20th December, 1355, he died, probably poisoned by his enemies.

One of the finest paintings, of which Serbia is justly proud, is that of Paja Jovanović, which depicts Stevan's coronation. Surrounded with Imperial splendour, he stands on the top of a flight of stairs, truest symbol of Serbian aspirations and of Serbian ideals.

Just think of it, how the whole of European history would have taken a different course *if* he had been successful in his last attempt to defeat Kantakouzene and drive the Turks back into Asia! *If* he had lived long enough to weld firmly together the loose confederacy of tribes he found on his accession and his conquests! It was not to be.

The Turks remained in Europe, and within a century they demolished the tumbling fabric of the Eastern Roman Empire. Stevan's Empire, too, declined under his successors. In 1371 the Turks in a decisive battle gained the victory and put part of Serbia under tribute. On June 15th (June 22nd, new style), 1389, Sultan Murat defeated the last independent Serbian ruler, Tsar Lazar, in the battle of Kosovo.

Shut in by a chain of mountains, and of vast extent, the plain of Kosovo seems intended by nature for an Armageddon of nations. "Amurath," says one of the Serbian national bards, " had so many men that a horseman could not ride from one wing of his army to the other in a fortnight; the plain of Kosovo was one mass of steel; horse stood against horse, man against man; the spears formed a thick forest; the banners obscured the sun; there was no space for a drop of water to fall between them." On the other side, Serbs, Bosnians, and Albanians were banded together in the common cause under Lazar's leadership.

Knolles, in his *History of the Turks* (1621 edition) tells us :—" In which bloodie fight many thousands fell on both sides; the brightness of the armour and weapons was as it had been the lightning; the multitude of launces and other horsemens staues shadowed the light of the sunne; arrowes and darts fell so fast that a man would have thought they had powred downe from heauen; the noise of the instruments of warre, with the neighing of horses, and outcries of men was so terrible and great, that the wild beasts of the mountains stood astonied therewith, and the Turkish histories, to expresse the terrour of the day (vainly say) that the Angels in heauen, amased with that hideous noise, for that time forgot the heauenly hymns wherewith they always glorifie God."

The struggle was furious on both sides, and Lazar held his own against the Ottoman forces. But there was treachery in the Serbian camp. Vuk Branković, to whom one wing of the Serbian army had been entrusted, had long been jealous of his sovereign. At a critical moment, when the future of the day was still undecided, the traitor turned

INTRODUCTION 27

his horse's head and rode off the field, followed by about 12,000 men. All was confusion in the Serbian ranks. Lazar's horse stumbled and fell, and his rider expired beneath the blows of the Turkish soldiers. According to another story, Lazar was captured, and beheaded in presence of the dying Sultan. With Lazar, his nine brothers-in-law and the flower of the Serbian arstocracy perished. Amurath was killed on the battlefield, after the actual fight was over, by Miloš, a brave Serbian. Vuk, the traitor, was poisoned a few years later by the next Sultan's order.

The Turks, however, had won the day. The defeat at Kosovo was an overwhelming national disaster for the Serbians. For more than four weary centuries they remained under the Turkish yoke.

And to-day?

Lazar's spirit still lives. Around the camp fires Serbian soldiers still recite the ballads that sing the deeds of their great ancestors. And before every Serbian's eyes arises that fine picture of Stevan Dušan, resplendent in his imperial robes. Spes mihi prima Deus!

ORIGIN AND AGE OF THE SERBIAN FOLK-SONGS

" Since the days of Homer's poems," so Jakob Grimm believes, " there has not been in Europe a phenomenon that, like the Serbian Folk-songs, can instruct us about the essence and origin of epic poetry." Various causes co operated to keep the spirit of popular poetry longer alive amongst the Serbians than in any other nation. There was the geographical isolation of the mountain-folk; the tenacity of their habits and customs, and their intolerance towards any interference or change; the obstinacy with which they clung to their language and religion; and, last but not least, the undoubted fact that the Turkish conqueror did not trouble himself very much about such matters as long as the taxes were paid.

That we do not know the authors of the folk-songs need not astonish us. Karadžić says:— "Amongst the people no one attaches the slightest importance to the actual composition of songs, and far from being proud of his work, the author of a song will deny being responsible for it and will put it on someone else. It is so even in the case of the most recent poetry, that of which one knows the place of origin, and which turns round some quite modern event; for hardly have a few days elapsed and no one bothers any longer about the origin and the author."

Some of the events and the heroes figuring in the Serbian heroic songs which have come down to us go back as far as the 12th century. Still older are probably the few obscure songs which contain traces of pagan rites. Frazer, in *The Golden Bough*, states:—" In time of drought the Serbians strip a girl to her skin and clothe her from head to foot in grass, herbs, and flowers, even her face being hidden behind a veil of living green. Thus disguised, she is called the Dodola, and goes through the village with a troop of girls. They stop before every house. The Dodola keeps turning herself round and dancing, while the other girls form a ring about her singing one of the Dodola songs, and the housewife pours a pail of water over her. One of the songs they sing runs thus:—

> We go through the village;
> The clouds go in the sky;
> We go faster,
> Faster go the clouds;
> They have overtaken us,
> And wetted the corn and the vine.

KARADŽIĆ

The Serbian folk-songs were for centuries known to the "common" people only, and were their production, their property. The few learned monks wrote biographies of fellow-scholars and the saints, or devoted themselves to feeble pseudo-classic imitations of the ancient or neighbouring literatures, and, worst of all, either wrote in Latin or in a monstrous jargon, in which the Serbian and Old Slavonic verbs were conjugated in the Russian fashion, and which was almost unintelligible with ugly loan words from other languages.

Apart from a few isolated attempts to collect some songs, it was only in the beginning of the 19th century that a beginning was made to compile them carefully and systematically. Vuk Stefanović Karadžić (1787-1864), a peasant's son and a great patriot, spent the whole of his life in collecting these treasures of his nation. At the same time—

in spite of scorn and ridicule—he succeeded in raising the popular dialect, the language of the common people, from the position of a despised slang to that of the standard literary language, and ultimately the dreadful hybrid jargon of the " classicists " had to go.

Karadžić wrote the first grammar of the Serbian language; he based its orthography on phonetic principles; he compiled a most excellent Serbian-German-Latin dictionary; and he wrote polemic pamphlets and dissertations without end. Justly he has been called " The father of Serbian modern literature."

But what interests us here more than anything else are his collections of the Serbian Folk-songs. The first collection appeared in 1814, comprising two small volumes; the last edition, published by the Serbian Government only some years ago, comprised nine big volumes.

Although Abbé Fortis, with his *Travels in Dalmatia*, and Herder, with his *Voices of the Nations*, were really the first in the field, it was by mere chance, and through the medium of German prose version that Gœthe, many years before 1814, had become acquainted with the fine poem Hasanaginica, and had published an excellent metrical version, thus introducing Serbian Folklore to the literature of the world. After Karadžić's work had appeared, Gœthe showed great interest in Serbian lore; he encouraged translators and used the columns of his *Ueber*

INTRODUCTION 31

Kunst und Altertum for appreciations and criticisms of the subject.

Grimm, a friend of Karadžić, translated some of the Folk-songs; he also rendered into German Karadžić's grammar, and wrote a preface to the Fairy-tales. Ranke, Kopitar, Laboulaye, Ami Boué, and Vater became Serbian enthusiasts.

But, like Luther, Karadžić, the Serbian reformer, was hated by the fanatics and the usual crowd of obscure old owls. The peasant's son, however, won the battle, and stopped the slow and pernicious process of de-nationalization. Karadžić died poor. In 1898 the remains of the great reformer were removed to the Cathedral in Belgrade.

Some of the songs Karadžić could write down, relying on the memories of his youth; for both his father and his grandfather had known many. Others he wrote at the dictation of blind old men, the Guslars, the only professional minstrels in Europe still in existence in the 19th century; others again he collected from peasants, pedlars, and Hajduks. These Hajduks were outlaws, men objecting to the Turkish misrule, men in reality hard and cruel, but at times as jolly as Robin Hood, and highly esteemed by the people. Sometimes it took several days before the conscientious collector managed to fix the text of a particularly long ballad, for the peasants were diffident and afraid he was fooling them; and some of the guslars developed a thirst as great as Marko's, and the aged minstrels' minds suffered slightly through the alliance between Bacchus and Calliope.

EXTERNAL INFLUENCES

The Folk-songs of the Serbians, like those of most other nations, have been under the influence of neighbours, of native and foreign customs and traditions much anterior to the time when the songs originated.

There are in the songs but few traces of the pagan cults before Christianity was introduced, though Fairy-tales, proverbs, and other Serbian folk-lore yield a richer harvest. Here we find snakes and dragons, witches, vampires, and werwolves; there are even echoes of the pest. The rain-making (Dodola) songs have already been mentioned. According to Talvj, there are in some of the love and wedding songs faint reminiscences of the old Serbian deities of Love.

A really interesting and typically Serbian phenomenon, however, is the Vila (plural, Vile). She is as beautiful as the Peri, though rather more wicked and malicious at times. She belongs to the family of the nymphs (θεαὶ Νύμφαι) and is even honoured with the epithet, " the cloud-gatherer " (Νεφεληγερέτα). Petrović tells us :—" The Serbian bards or troubadours from the early fourteenth century to our day have ever glorified and sung of the Vile, describing them as very beautiful and eternally young, robed in the whitest and finest gauze, with shimmery golden hair flowing down over snow-white bosoms. Vile were said to have very sweet voices, and sometimes to be armed with bows and arrows. Their melodious songs were often heard on the borders of the lakes or in the meadows

INTRODUCTION

hidden deep in the forests, or on high mountain-peaks." In some cases a Vila seems to have taken up the position of a guardian-angel, and attached herself to one particular human being. Thus we read of the Vila who came to Marko, telling him of his impending death. The Vila's speed was extraordinary, and many passages in the folk-songs descriptive of her flight rival the lines in Lalla Rookh :—

> " Rapidly as comets run
> To th' embraces of the sun ;—
> Fleeter than the starry brands
> Flung at night from angel hands
> At those dark and daring sprites
> Who would climb th' empyreal heights."

Of other superstitions " there is ample abundance in Serbian folk-lore. In fact, in Serbia, as in most other countries, there is still a large task before Knowledge, the fair sister of Freedom, before Tennyson's distant golden dream is realized, till every Soul be free !"

On Mid-summer Eve the herdsmen light torches and march round the sheep-folds and cattle-stalls. " Nowhere in Europe," says Frazer, " is the old heathen ritual of the Yule log preserved to the present day more perfectly than in Serbia; the children and young people go from home to home singing special songs called Colleda, because of an old pagan divinity, who is invoked in every line. In one of them she is spoken of as a beautiful little maid; in another she is implored to make the cows yield milk abundantly." We hear that :—" Even to-day Serbian peasants believe that eclipses of the sun and moon are caused by their becoming the prey of a hungry dragon, who tries to swallow them."

In the fairy-tales the "external soul" figures several times. Peculiar is the fact that some fairy-tales are more or less identical with stories of ancient Greek lore. A giant-fool appears in a fairy-tale, which differs but slightly from the story of Polyphemos; we come across the story about the long ass's ears of King Midas; the idea of a war between Justice and Injustice as perceived by Deioces in Herodotus has its parallel in a fairy-tale given in this collection. I have been much interested in discovering in the "Gesta Romanorum" several points of contact and parallels, and in a few cases obvious "loans." Both the marriage trial à la Brunhilde, a race in "The Maiden Swifter than a Horse," and the method of impeding a running girl in "The Wonderful Hair," are to be found in the "Gesta Romanorum" ("De avaritia et ejus subtili conamine").

The historical events brought about by contact with the Turks, Venice, and Hungary had, of course, the greatest possible influence, which finds clear expression in a very great number of songs.

Special attention should perhaps be drawn here to the influence of Turkish civilization, as shown in "Hasanaginica." The poem (page 64) has a Serbian-Turkish milieu. The difficulty of the reader has perhaps been best stated and met by the words of a distinguished young Serbian scholar, M. Curčin. He says:—"The difficulty which perplexes the West-European educated reading public when judging the line of conduct in the poem and at the same time the *sine quâ non* of the whole of the conflict consists in the relationship existing between married people amongst Orientals, especially the Mahomedans, in the low status and almost slavish submissiveness of the Oriental woman towards her husband. The most important item, the one on which the greatest emphasis should be laid, is the sense of shame itself—quite incomprehensible for us in such a degree—shown by the married woman towards her husband." The classic poem given on page 64 of this collection may be called a real tragedy—defining tragedy as a conflict not between good and evil, not between right and wrong, but between right and right. Curčin, therefore, appropriately calls the poem " a drama, the tragic fate of a loving wife and mother, her soul's struggle with the brute force of circumstances."

CLASSIFICATION AND SUBJECTS TREATED

The Serbian Folk-songs have been divided into Men's Songs and Women's Songs. The latter are of a more lyrical, the former of a narrative, epic character.

Karadžić says:—" Our popular poetry consists of heroic songs which the men sing, or rather recite, with the accompaniment of the guslé, and of domestic songs which are mostly sung by women and maidens, but also by men, especially by young men. Those who sing the women's songs do so for their own amusement, whereas the heroic poems are chiefly intended for the audience; that is the reason why so much regard is paid in the former to the musical part and in the latter to poetic expression."

The women's songs have even stanzas at times and various metres, whereas the men's songs, without exception, are written in decasyllabic verse, and have neither rhyme nor assonance.

The lyrical songs are, in the words of Gœthe, " very beautiful indeed." There is little doubt that in purity, gracefulness, and roguish fancies these songs are almost unique. It is true the maidens do not mince words if they are angry or jealous, and their imprecations and curses on faithless lovers are worthy of Dido's passion. Yet one cannot but agree with the critic that the Serbian women's songs taken as a whole, " grown up on the borders between Orient and Occident, combine the advantages of the lyric poetry of both. The thoughts are more violent, more highly coloured than in the folk-songs of the rest of Europe, and yet there is nothing of the bombast and hypersensitiveness of Arabian and Persian poetry. Their charming fragrance does not dull the senses. Theirs is the perfume of roses, but not that of the attar of roses."

The heroic songs deal mostly with the deeds and adventures of the great Serbians of the past. Voyages to Italy, to the lands of the Arabs, *i.e.*, both the Moors and the Negroes, magnificent banquets and weddings, and furious battles, form the regular topics. The passionate hatred of the Turks and the furious battles with the Turkish hosts are amongst the most frequent and regular designs in their poetic texture.

In the gallery of fierce, almost savage, super-men of the past, Marko Kraljević holds the first place. He belongs to the family of the Hercules, Cid, Roland, Siegfried, and Gargantua. The historic Marko, a contemporary and rival of Tsar Lazar, was very far from being just what one would expect a national hero to be; but popular imagination, forgetting or disregarding his shortcomings, overlaying the historical figure with the capricious fancies and idealizing traits of which every National Muse is so fond, raised him to the proud position of Serbia's symbol of freedom, the embodiment of her ineradicable hatred of the Turks.

A great number of poems enlarge on Marko's adventures. Almost as famous as he is his faithful horse Šarac, a gallant charger as courageous and thirsty as his master.

The battle of Kosovo holds almost the same place of honour, but fewer poems, some indeed only fragmentary, have come down to us. Several attempts have been made to weld all the Kosovo songs and fragments together into one organic structure, which, if some future Serbian genius should succeed in performing the almost impossible task, might well be considered another Iliad.

METRE

The sounds of the Serbian language are so melodious, so soft and pleasing, that Serbian has been called the Italian amongst the Slavonic languages.

It has a great variety of accentuation and intonation, but this intonation and the accent of the spoken language disappears almost absolutely in verse. Its place is taken by a conventional and measured pronunciation.

Thus we find in the Men's Songs the Serbian Heroic Metre. Each line consists of five trochaic feet, usually divided by a caesure after the fourth syllable. Each line as a rule is complete in itself as a sense group; but very often, as in Hindoo poetry, the lines run in couples (that is, the second completes the meaning of the first, even although the first taken by itself may appear to present a complete sense); enjambment never occurs at all.

The following line of Serbian words, if one takes them singly and isolated, would have such quantities as indicated (— denoting a long and accentuated syllable; ∪, a short syllable without accent).

$$\underset{\text{I}}{\cup} \underset{\text{ponese}}{- \cup \cup} \mid \underset{\text{tri}}{-} \underset{\text{tovara}}{- \cup \cup} \underset{\text{blaga}}{- \cup}$$

but when recited or sung as a metrical structure the verse would scan :—

$$\underset{\text{I}}{-} \underset{\text{ponese}}{\cup - \cup} \mid \underset{\text{tri}}{-} \underset{\text{tovara}}{\cup - \cup} \underset{\text{blaga}}{- \cup}$$

It is this peculiar shifting of the accents used in colloquial speech for the purpose of poetical diction which can be observed in the Serbian language, that may throw some light on the vexed question about the relation between accent and quantity in ancient Greek prosody. "In modern poetry, Accent is the basis of Rhythm. In old Greek poetry, Quantity is the basis of Rhythm, and Accent has no influence which we can perceive" (Jebb). It is hardly to be assumed that the ancient Greeks invented such ample means of accent-notation for nothing. Modern Greek has a strongly marked accent. Is it not highly probable that the notation of accents observed in daily life and colloquial speech was disregarded, just as in Serbian? Two lines taken from Œdipus Tyrannus (151, 159) and treated as the one Serbian line above will perhaps best illustrate this hypothesis :—

ὦ Διὸς ἀδυεπὲς φάτι, τίς ποτε τᾶς πολυχρύσου
— ∪ ∪ — ∪ ∪ — ∪ ∪ — ∪ ∪ — ∪ ∪ — —
ω Δι ος | α δυ επ | ες φατι ‖ τις ποτε | τας πολυ | χρ υσου.

or,

πρῶτά σε κεκλόμενος. θύγατερ Διὸς ἄμβροτ' Ἀθάνα
— ∪ ∪ — ∪ ∪ — ∪ ∪ — ∪ ∪ — ∪ ∪ — —
πρωτα σε | κεκλομεν | ος θυγατ ‖ ερ Διος | αμβρο τ Αθ | ανα.

Certain writers on Serbian prosody, however, hold that their heroic verse does not consist of five trochees; that perhaps such an analysis of the metrical structure is only permissible as a practicable handle and method for dealing with Serbian versification, but that in reality the Serbian folk-poet merely counts ten syllables without measuring them, and that actually the line is "without any fixed fall or tonality." But the cadence of the Serbian heroic verse, its general modulation, does seem to be, on the whole, of a trochaic or dactylic character.

In the Women's Songs we find a greater variety of metre, the metrical structure is sometimes more complex, and stanzas occur in many of the lyrical poems.

MUSIC

The division of Serbian Folk-songs into Men's Songs and Women's Songs determines not only the subject-matter and the metre, but also the character of the music accompanying the songs.

Prince Lazarović Hrebelianović says:—" The Serbian epic poems are always chanted, accompanied by the guslé. They are recitations in rhythmic declamation; the motif of the melody suggested is fragmentary, and runs within three or four notes. Each note is divided into fractions of tones, fixed in the execution and learned by ear, which cannot be transcribed on the modern musical staff. The cadences are grave and evocative, droning, yet vibrating as if on human heart-strings."

The music accompanying the recital of the epic poems certainly is simple and rather monotonous; there is no strict adherence to "time" or "scale." In some parts of Serbia the guslar strikes his one-stringed instrument, the guslé, with his bow of horse-hair during the whole of his recital; in other parts the string is usually only struck at the end of each line.

The guslé is made by the peasants from the wood

of a species of maple tree (acer platanoides Linn.); the piece of wood is scooped out and covered with sheep-skin. The player rests the instrument on his knees and plays—somewhat like a violoncello—by means of an arc-shaped bow. The guslé is the national instrument. A modern Serbian poet writes:—

" It has been said,
 The house in which the guslé is not heard,
 That house is dead.
 It has been said,
 The man whose heart no guslé has yet stirred,
 That man is dead!"

The lyrical poems are musically superior to the Men's Songs, though the slow and languorous rhythm of the music accompanying them somehow palls on the Western ear after a time. " When rendered according to modern harmony," says Lazarović, " they are either in suspense or half-finished."
The Women's Songs are mostly sung in connection with the Kolo, the national dance. " Kolo " means the " wheel " or " circle." It is a round dance, danced in the open. In the middle of the circle is the music; usually one bagpipe will do, but an oaten-pipe, a drum, and another bagpipe are added occasionally. Very often the musicians join in the dance. The ring-dance sways from the right to the left, and then again from the left to the right. Meanwhile the text is sung twice (Cf. Appendix, pages 162-167). Sometimes the singer acts as pre-

centor, and the choir follows the lead or repeats. Only when the melody sung with the text comes to an end does the instrumental music set in, and refrains are often sung at the same time.

CONCLUSION

About a century has passed since the Folk-songs of Serbia were introduced to the literary public. Those who followed up a slight acquaintance and became on friendly terms with the Muse of the Mountains, have been untiring in their praise of the Serbian Folk-songs for their beauty, their classical naiveté, and their subdued Oriental colouring. The fascination these poems exercise becomes stronger as the years go by, and since contemporary eminent scholars, like P. Popović, F. S. Krauss, and others, are constantly adding to our knowledge and appreciation, it is to be hoped that the whole of Europe will soon become acquainted with the Folk-songs of Serbia.

They are the songs about which a German critic ("Göttinger Gelehrte Anzeigen," 1823) said:—"The perusal of these songs, yea, their mere existence, must impress upon the unbiassed reader that a nation which sings, thinks, and acts as the Serbian, should not be allowed to bear the name of a subjected nation!" Ceterum censeo . . . !

FOLK SONGS

" The wealth and the beauty of Serbian Folk-songs are such as to astonish Europe."

J. GRIMM

CEASE THY WARBLINGS, NIGHTINGALE!

O nightingale! thy warblings cease,
And let my master sleep in peace:
'Twas I who lull'd him to repose,
And I will wake him from his rest;
I'll seek the sweetest flower that grows,
And bear it to his presence blest;
And gently touch his cheeks, and say,
" Awake, my master! for 'tis day."

THE MAIDEN AND THE VIOLET

Little violet, drooping all alone, like my own
Drooping heart, I would pluck thee; but there's none, no not one!
To whom I dare to give thee: so I leave thee and pass on.
I would give thee gladly, gladly, if I dared, to Ali Bey;
But too proud (ah, well-a-day) is Ali Bey—so they say!
Proud he is! I do not dare. Would he care, he, to wear
Any flower that buds or blows? . . . save the rose, I suppose!
No! rest there, and despair! Live or die! Thou and I
Have no chance to catch one glance from his eye passing by.

SOLICITUDE

I fain would sing—but will be silent now,
For pain is sitting on my lover's brow;
And he would hear me—and, though silent, deem
I pleased myself, but little thought of him,
While of naught else I think; to him I give
My spirit—and for him alone I live:
Bear him within my heart, as mothers bear
The last and youngest object of their care.

SPRING SONG

The winter is gone,
    Beloved, arise!
The spring is come on,
The birds are all singing,
    Beloved, arise!

The roses are springing,
Earth laughs out in love:
    Beloved, arise!
And thou, my sweet dove!
O waste not thy time:
    Beloved, arise!

Enjoy the sweet bliss
Of thy lover's fond kiss:
    Beloved, arise!
In the hour of thy prime,
    Beloved, arise!

THE ABSENT LOVER

(See pages 162-3.)

Gloomy night! how full art thou of darkness!
Thou, my heart! art fuller yet of sorrow,
Sorrow which I bear, but cannot utter!
I have not a mother to console me,
I have not a sister who might sooothe me,—
I have but a friend—and he is absent!
Ere he comes, the night will be departed;
Ere he wakes, the birds will sing their matins;
Ere he kisses, twilight comes and tells him,
Go thy way, my friend! the day is dawning.

THE MAIDEN AND THE TALISMAN

His breath is amber,—sharp his reed,
The hand which holds it, snowy white,*
He writes fair talismans,—a creed
For maidens doth the loved one write:
" Of him that will not have thee—think not!
From him that fain would have thee—shrink not."

---

* " White " is a standing epithet denoting beauty, constantly used in popular Serbian poetry.

CARES AND CURSES

Thou heavenly spirit! kindly tell me,
   Where tarries now this youth of mine;
Is he a wanderer, wandering ever,
   Or doth he linger drinking wine?

If he be speeding on, a wanderer
   With joy and gladness let him be:
If quaffing wine, in quiet seated,
   O! his be peace and gaiety!

But if he love another maiden,
   Dost thou think I shall care? Oh, no!
Yet be his heart with anguish laden!
   And let Heaven smite his path with woe!

LONGINGS

O that I were a little stream,
That I might flow to him—to him!
How I should dance with joy, when knowing
To whom my sparkling wave was flowing!
Beneath his window would I glide,
And linger there till morning-tide;
Then should he weak or thirsty be,
Perhaps he'd stoop to drink of me!
Or baring there his bosom, lave
That bosom in my rippling wave.

THE UNHAPPY BRIDE

(See pages 166-7.)

The maiden gave the ring she wore
To him who gave it her before:
" O take the ring,—for thou and thine
Are hated,—not by me,—but mine:—
Father and mother will not hear thee,
Brother and sister both forswear thee:
Yet, think not, youth,—O think not ill
Of her who needs must love thee still!
I am a poor unhappy maid,
Whose path the darkest clouds o'ershade;
I sowed sweet basil, and there grew
On that same spot the bitterest rue:
And wormwood, that unholy flower,
Is now alone my marriage dower;
The only flower which they shall wear
Who to the maiden's marriage come,
When for my marriage altar there
The guests shall find the maiden's tomb.

REMEMBRANCE

O! if I were a mountain streamlet,
   I know where I would flow;
I'd spring into the crystal Sava,
   Where the gay vessels go,
That I might look upon my lover—
   For fain my heart would know

If, when he holds the helm, he ever
  Looks on my rose, and thinks
Of her who gave it;—if the nosegay
  I made of sweetest pinks
Is faded yet, if he still wears it.

  Such flowers beautiful
I culled and bound last Saturday,
  And when I said Good-bye,
For sweet remembrance gave him them on Sunday.

FROZEN HEART

Thick fell the snow upon St. George's day;
  The little birds all left their cloudy bed;
The maiden wandered barefoot on her way;
  Her brother bore her sandals, and he said:
" O, sister mine, cold, cold thy feet must be."
  " No! not my feet, sweet brother! not my feet—
But my poor heart is cold with misery.
  There's nought to chill me in the snowy sleet:
My mother—'tis my mother who hath chilled me,
Bound me to one who with disgust hath filled me."

DESPAIR

How I am tortured!
Sleepless all night,
Suffering ever,
Death in my heart:
For my beloved
Soon I shall die!

RETALIATION

Lo! the maiden greets the Day-star: "Sister!
Sister! Star of Morning! well I greet thee;
Thou dost watch the world from thine uprising
To thy sinking hour. In Hercgovina
Tell me, didst thou see the princely Stevan?
Tell me, was his snowy palace open,
Were his steeds caparisoned and ready,
And was he equipp'd his bride to visit?"

Gently then the Morning Star responded:
"Lovely sister! beautiful young maiden,
True, I watch the world from my uprising
To my setting;—and in Hercgovina
Saw the palace of the princely Stevan;
And that snowy palace was wide open,
And his horse was saddled, and was ready,
And he was equipp'd his bride to visit:
But not thee—not thee—another maiden;
False tongues three have whispered evil of thee;
One has said—thine origin is lowly;
One, thou art as treacherous as a serpent;
And the third, that thou art dull and dreamy."

Then the maiden pour'd her imprecations:
"He who said my origin was lowly,
Never let a child of love be born him;
He who called me treacherous as a serpent,
Coiling round his heart a serpent subtle
Through hot summers in his hair be tangled,
Through cold winters in his bosom nestle;
He who dared to call me dull and dreamy,

Nine long years may he be worn with sickness,
And no sleep renew his strength to bear it."

THE PALE HAG JEALOUSY

Fairest youths are here—but not the fairest!
Would that I could hear him now or see him,
Just to know if he be sick, or faithless!
Were he sick, my ears would rather hear it,
Than the rumour of some other maiden.
Sickness may depart, and time restore him,—
But he never will return if faithless.

LOVE AND SLEEP

I walked the high and hollow woods, from dawn to even-dew,
The wild-eyed woods they stared on me, unclasped, and let me through,
Where mountain pines, like great black birds, stood perched against the blue.

Not a whisper heaved the woven woof of those warm trees:
All the little leaves lay flat, unmoved by bird or breeze:
Day was losing light all round, by indolent degrees.

Underneath the brooding branches, all in holy shade,
Unseen hands of mountain things a mossy couch had made:

There asleep among pale flowers my beloved was laid.

Slipping down, a sunbeam bathed her brows with bounteous gold,
Unmoved upon her maiden breast her heavy hair was rolled,
Her smile was still as though she died while of my love I told.

"O God!" I thought, "if this be death, that makes no sound nor stir!"
My heart stood still with tender awe, I dared not waken her,
But to the dear God, in the sky, this prayer I did prefer:

"Grant, dear Lord, in the blessed sky, a warm wind from the sea,
To shake a leaf down on my love from yonder leafy tree;
That she may open her sweet eyes, and haply look on me."

A little wind from the distant sea arrived at God's behest,
It shook a leaflet from the tree, and laid it on her breast;
Her sweet eyes ope'd and looked on me.—How can I tell the rest?

THE MAIDEN'S APPEAL

Grazing on the dewy pastures green
Stood my snow-white steed and listened fondly
To my sweetheart pleading with her mother:
" Do not make me marry him I love not,
Rather would I go into the forest
With the one I love and live on hawthorn,
Draw us water with a leaf, and rather
Would I sleep upon a stone as pillow
Than on silk to rest in lofty mansions,
Live on sweetmeats with the man I love not!"

THE LOVER'S BLESSING

(See pages 164-5.)

The wild hawk sat the dark night long
    Beside the window of Milan,
And ever and anon her song
    Thus sharp and clear began :—

" Rise up, it is a noble feast,
    Thine own true love to-night doth wed;
Rise, taste the cup, or send at least
    Thy blessing to the bed."

Milan made answer : " By my word,
    To drink her wine I will not go;
But thou shalt hear my blessing, bird,
    Since thou wilt have it so :

May for each drop this night she drains
   Ten thousand tears hereafter flow !
Be child-birth pains the only pains
   That bed shall never know !"

LOVE AND DIGNITY

HE : " Violet, little one mine !
   I would love thee, but thou art so small."

SHE : " Love me, my love, from those heights of thine,
And I shall grow tall, so tall !
The pearl is small, but it hangs above
A royal brow, and a kingly mind :
The quail is little, little, my love,
But she leaves the hunter behind."

SURRENDER

HE : O maiden, vermeil rose !
Unplanted, unsown,
Blooming alone
As the wild-flower blows,
With a will of thine own !
Neither grafted nor grown,
Neither gathered nor blown,
O maiden, O rose !
Blooming alone
In the green garden close,

Unnoticed, unknown,
Unpropt, unsupported,
Unwatered, unfed,
Unkissed and uncourted,
Unwooed and unwed,
O sweet wild rose,
Who knows? who knows?
Might I kiss thee and court thee?
My kiss would not hurt thee!
O sweet, sweet rose,
In the green garden-close!
If a gate were undone,
And if I might come to thee,
And meet thee alone?
Sue thee and woo thee,
And make thee my own?
Clasp thee and cull thee,—
What harm would be done?

SHE : Beside thy field my garden blows,
Were a gate in the garden left open . .
    who knows?
And I watered my garden at eventide?
Who knows?
And if somebody silently happened to ride
That way? And a horse to the gate should
    be tied?
And if somebody (who knows who?) unespied,
Were to enter my garden to gather a rose?
Who knows? . . . . . . I suppose
No harm need be done. My belovèd one,
Come lightly, come softly, at set of the sun.
Come and caress me!

Kiss me and press me!
Fold me and hold me!
Kiss me with kisses that leave not a trace,
And set not the print of thy teeth on my face,
Or my mother will see it and scold me.

THE HUNTER'S PRIZE

On my farm the dawn of day did find me,
At the chase the early sun when risen,
I upon the mountain—he behind it.
On that mountain, by a dark-green pine tree,
Lo! I saw a lovely maiden sleeping:
On a clover-sheaf her head was pillowed;
On her bosom lay two snowy dovelets,
In her lap there was a dappled fawkin.
There I tarried till the fall of evening:
Bound my steed at night beneath the pine-tree:
Bound my falcon to the pine-tree branches:
Gave the sheaf of clover to my courser:
Gave the two white dovelets to my falcon:
Gave the dappled fawkin to my greyhound:
And to me,—I took the lovely maiden.

REMINISCENCE

HE: "And art thou wed, my Beloved?
My Beloved of long ago!"

SHE: "I am wed, my Beloved. And I have given
A child to the world of woe.
And the name I have given the child is thine:
So that, when I call to me my little one,

The heaviness of this heart of mine
For a little while may be gone.
For I say not . . . 'Hither, hither, my son!'
But . . . 'Hither, my Love, my Beloved!'"

KEEPSAKES

Was it a vine, with clusters white,
   That clung round Budim's stateliest tower?
O no, it was a lady bright,
That hung upon an armèd knight,—
   It was their parting hour.

They had been wedded in their youth;
   Together they had spent their bloom;
That hearts so long entwined in truth
Asunder should be torn in ruth,
   It was a cruel doom.

"Go forth," she said; "pursue thy way;
   But some fair garden shouldst thou see,
Alone among the arbours stray,
And pluck a rose-bud from the spray,
   The freshest there may be;

Unclasp thy mail, when none is by,
   That bud upon thy breast to lay,
How soon 'twill wither, fade, and die,
Observe—for that poor bud am I,
   From thee, my stem, away."

"And thou, my soul," the soldier said,
   "When I am wandering, faint and far,

Go thou to our own greenwood shade,
Where I the marble fountain made,
  And placed the golden jar.

At noon I filled my jar with wine,
  And dropp'd therein a ball of snow,
Lay that on this warm heart of thine,
And while it melts behold me pine
  In solitary woe."

MERRIMENT

Through the mountain-forest
  Comes a merry boy;
In her lovely garden
  Strolls a maiden coy.
He with hawthorn berries
  Pelts her fair soft cheeks;
Quick with fruit of blackthorn
  Sweet revenge she seeks.
Neither youth nor maiden
  Harm or hurt intend;
Love and love's caresses,—
  This is what they send.

LOVE'S TRIAL

Thirty sturdy fellows from Cetinje
Seated near the cool and quiet river,
Quaffed their wine and teased the pretty maiden
Who supplied their ever empty goblets.
Bolder than the rest, some tried to kiss her,

But the maiden from Cetinje told them,
" Though a waitress to you all, my fellows,
Sweetheart am I but to him who ventures
For my sake to swim this mighty river;
Let him take his sword and all his armour;
Furthermore, I wish that on his shoulders
He shall wear this precious velvet mantle.
Thus from bank to bank the hero-swimmer
Cross the river, and on his returning
I will be his faithful wife for ever!"

But for one, the thirty valiant warriors
Looked shamefacèdly into their goblets.
He, however, dared her, leaped up quickly,
Donned his armour, took his sword, the mantle
Heavy as a coronation garment,
Dived into the river, swam across it,
Touched the other bank just with his sword-point;
Then returned, but all at once—went under!
Not that suddenly his strength had failed him,
No! he swam below the water's surface
That he might find out his love's devotion.
When the maiden from Cetinje saw it,
With a cry of anguish she ran forwards
Straight into the river to her lover
Radoiza. Then the daring swimmer
Grasped her firmly by the hands, and with her
Gained the land where his companions cheered him.
Soon he led away with him the maiden,
Now the mistress of his white-hued homestead.

THE KNITTER

The maiden sat upon the hill,
Upon the hill and far away,
Her fingers wove a silken cord,
And thus I heard the maiden say:
" O, with what joy, what ready will,
If some fond youth, some youth adored,
Might wear thee, should I weave thee now!
The finest gold I'd interblend,
The richest pearls as white as snow.
But if I knew, my silken friend,
That some old fool should wear thee, Fye!
The coarsest hemp I would inweave,
The finest silk for sedge-grass leave,
And all thy knots with nettles tie."

MAY AND DECEMBER

I heard young Falisava* say:
" I'll have no ancient greybeard, nay!
A sprightly beardless youth for me!"
An aged man the maiden heard,
He shaves his long and snowy beard,
Paints his moustache like ebony:
To Falisava then he goes—
" My heart! my soul! my sweetest rose!
A beardless youth is come for thee."
And then she listened—they were wed—
And to the old man's home they sped.

  * Serbian word for " boastful."

Then twilight came, and evening's shade—
" Now," said the old man to the maid :
" Sweet Falisava ! maiden fair !
Our bed beside the stove prepare
And the warm feather mattress bear."—
The maiden heard, the maiden went
And gathered flowers of sweetest scent,
Of sweetest scent and fairest hue,
Which on the old man's bed she threw,
And like a strong-wing'd eagle then
Flew to her father's home again.

ALL'S WELL THAT ENDS WELL

On the hill, the fir-tree hill,
    Grows a tall fir-tree :
There a maiden, calm and still,
    Sits contentedly.
To a youthful swain she pledges
    Vows : " O, come to me :
Lightly spring across the hedges,
    Come—but silently.
Come at eve, lest harm betide thee,
    Come—my home to seek.
In our quiet dwelling hide thee ;
    Not a whisper speak."

As he o'er the hedges leapt,
    Lo ! a twig he tore :
Stealthily he crawled and crept,
    Noisy was that door.
When he entered, bang ! there fell

Crockery on the floor,
Then her mother comes afeard,
Trips and cuts her knee;
And her father burns his beard
In perplexity.
But the boy puts out the flame,
And thus wins the game.

THE ROGUISH MAIDEN

Lepota* went out to the harvest—to wield
A sickle of silver in fingers of gold;†
And the sun mounted high o'er the parch'd harvest
   field,
From her throat white as snow sweetest melodies
   rolled:—
" I'll give my white forehead to him who shall bind
All the sheaves which my sickle leaves scattered
   behind;
I'll give my black eyes to the friend who shall bring
A draught of sweet water just fresh from the spring;
And to him who shall bear me to rest in the shade,
I will be—and for aye—an affectionate maid."

And she thought that her words were all wasted in
   air;
But a shepherd, just watching his sheep-fold, was
   there,
And he flew, and with sedges he bound all the
   sheaves,

   * Serbian word for Beauty.
   † " Gold " and " golden " denote beauty and strength.

And he made her an arbour of hazelwood leaves;
And he ran to the spring and he brought the sweet
    water,
And he looked on the face of Beauty's young
    daughter.
And he said, "Lovely maiden, thy promise I
    claim;"
But the maiden was roguish and playing a game.
And she said to the shepherd, all blushing, "No!
    no!
Go back to thy sheep-fold, thou wanderer, go!
For if thou didst bind the loose sheaves, thou has
    left
Thy sheep in the stubble to wander bereft;
And if from the fountain a draught thou has
    brought,
Dost thou reckon thy share of its coolness for
    naught?
And if thou hast reared up an arbour of shade,
For thyself as for me its refreshment was made."

HASANAGINICA.

What's so white upon yon verdant forest?
Snow perhaps it is or swans assembled?
Snow would surely long ago have melted,
And a flight of swans would have departed.
No! not swans, not snow it is you see there,
'Tis the tent of Aga, Hasan Aga;
On his couch he lies, severely wounded,

And his mother seeks him, and his sister,
But for very shame his wife is absent.*

When the misery of his wounds was softened,
Hasan thus his faithful wife commanded:
" In my house thou shalt abide no longer—
Thou shalt dwell no more among my kindred."
When his wife had heard this awful sentence,
Numbed with dread she stood and full of sorrow.
When outside she heard the tramp of horses,
To the highest window of the tower
Rushed the faithful Hasanaginica,
Would have thrown herself into the courtyard,
But her two belovèd daughters followed,
Crying after her in tearful anguish—
" Do come back to us, oh, mother, mother!
These are not our father Hasan's coursers,
'Tis our uncle Pintorovich coming."

Then, returning, Hasanaginica
Threw her arms in misery round her brother—
" See the sorrow, brother, of thy sister:
He would tear me from my helpless children."

He was silent—but from out his pocket,
Safely wrapped in silk of deepest scarlet,
Letters of divorce he drew, and bid her

* In Serbian households it was not usual for the wife to enter her husband's presence unless summoned by himself. Hasan Aga, however, seemed to have expected that, under present circumstances, his wife would have broken through all conventional etiquette in order to tend him, and to have unjustly regarded her failure to do so as denoting a grievous lack of love for him. (*Cf. Introduction, p.* 34-5.)

E

Seek again her agèd mother's dwelling—
Free to win and wed another husband.

When she saw the letter of divorcement,
Parting-kisses on her two boys' foreheads,
On her girls' red cheeks she pressed in sorrow.
But she could not tear herself from baby
Crowing at his mother from the cradle.
But at last her brother with an effort
Tore the mother from her tender infant,
Put her close behind him on his courser,
Hastened with her to the white-hued homestead.
But a short while dwelt she with her people—
Not a single week had been completed,
When a host of suitors wooed the lady
Of a noble family the flower;
One of them Imoski's mighty Cadi.
Said the noble lady, trembling greatly,
" I entreat thee, I implore thee, brother,
Do not give me to another husband.
For the sight of my poor orphan'd children
Sure would break the spirit of thy sister!"

Little cared her brother for her sorrows;
He had sworn she should espouse the Cadi.
Then his sister asked of him a favour:
" Write on snow-white paper, O, my brother,
To the Cadi as a bridal message,
' Friendly greetings from the youthful woman,
And she begs thee bring her as a present,
When thy wedding-guests and thou art coming
Hither to her peoples' white-hued homestead,
Such a long and flowing veil that passing
Aga's home she need not see her orphans.'

When the snow-white letter reached the Cadi,
All his wedding-guests he called together,
And set out with them for his betrothèd,
Future mistress of his white-hued homestead.
Safely reached he with his friends her dwelling;
Happily were all returning homeward,
But when they were passing Aga's homestead,
Her two daughters saw her from the window,
Her two sons came out, and from the portal
Called to her, " Come hither! O, come hither!
Take thy night's repast with thine own children!"

Sadly Hasanaginica heard them;
And she said to him who led the party,
" I should be most grateful to you, captain,
If you kindly halted the procession
While I give some presents to the children."

So they stopped at the belovèd portal,
Presents gave she unto all the children.
To the boys, high boots with gold embroidered;
To the girls, long and resplendent dresses;
And a silken garment to her baby.—

Near them sat their father, Hasan Aga,
And he called in sorrow to his children,
" Come to me, poor children! to your father,
From your mother do not hope for pity,
Callous is she, cold and stony-hearted."
Hasanaginica, when she heard this,
On the ground she fell all pale and trembling,
And her spirit left its earthly prison
At the glances of her orphan children.

HAJKUNA'S MARRIAGE

Never, never, since the world's beginning,
Never, never, bloomed a fairer blossom
Than was reared of late beneath the shadow
Of the noble Ljubović's fastness.
White and high o'er Nevesinje looking
Stands the tower wherein they reared Hajkuna,
But it holds no more the flower of beauty,—
Far away is Ljubović's sister.

Fair she was, there could be nothing fairer;
Stately was she as the mountain pine-tree;
White and rosy-colour intermingled
On her cheeks, as though the dawn had kissed her;
Dark and flashing, like two noble jewels,
Were her eyes; and over them were eyebrows
Thin and black like leeches* from the fountain;
Dark the lashes too; although the ringlets
Hung above in clusters rich and golden;
Softer were her eyelids than the pinions
Of the swallow on the breeze reposing.
Sweeter were the maiden's lips than honey;
White her teeth, as pearls in ocean ripen'd;
White her breasts, two little panting wild doves;
Soft her speaking, as the wild dove's murmur;
Bright her smiling as the burst of sunshine.
Wide through Bosnia and Hercegovina
Went the story of her wondrous beauty.

* This is a somewhat strange, but very frequent, simile in Serbian poetry.

Lovers many came about the maiden;
Two above the rest came late and early;
One, the hoary-bearded Mustaf-Aga,
Lord of Krajina, of Castle-Novo.
Mustaf-Aga, at her brother's portal,
As the sun went down on Nevesinja,
Met another that was come a-wooing,
Young and noble Zuko of Udbinja.

Mustaf-Aga brought a thousand pieces
Purest gold upon a golden basin;
Round the basin twined a golden serpent—
Eyes of diamond glittered in its forehead,
Eyes of diamond, glittering so splendid
Men might feast at midnight by their shining.
Zuko offered but a dozen ducats,
All he had he offered for the maiden;
Lord was he of little but his sabre,
And a powerful white-coloured charger.
Noble Zuko made the border feed him,
As the air is fain to feed the falcon.

Ljubović then spake unto his sister,
" See, my sister, see my dear Hajkuna,
In the hour in which thy mother bore thee
It was written somebody should wed thee;
Many lovers came to me a-wooing,
But this night the two that are the noblest
Are both here, within the court together.
Here is hoary-bearded Mustaf-Aga,
Come from Krajina, his Castle-Novo;
Untold wealth hath lordly Mustaf-Aga,
All in silk and satin would he clothe thee,

Every day with honey would he feed thee.
Close beside is Zuko of Udbinja;
Lord is he of little but his sabre,
And a powerful white-coloured charger.
Choose, Hajkuna, choose to-night, my sister,
Choose and tell me which of them shall wed thee."

Then the sister spake unto her brother,
" Thine the choice is, thine alone, my brother;
He to whom thou givest me is my husband.
But for me, I'd rather have a bridegroom
Young and bold and true, though without treasures,
Than the richest who is hoary-bearded.
Wealth, it is not gold, it is not silver;
Wealth is to possess what most we cherish."

And Ljubović heard his sister's answer,
Yet he gave the maid to Mustaf-Aga;
Sore against her will he gave Hajkuna.
Mustaf-Aga swiftly rode to Novo;
Mustaf bade his kinsmen to the wedding;
Zuko too was asked by Mustaf-Aga—
Noble Zuko was to ride as leader
With the banner, bringing home the maiden.
Richly clad came Mustaf-Aga's kindred;
Then they rode to Ljubović's fastness.

White days three they feasted in the fastness;
But they mounted early in the morning,
Then they led her from her brother's dwelling.
When her home lay far behind the maiden
Far within the plain of Nevesinje,
Fair Hajkuna whispered to the bridesman,

" Tell me, kinsman, tell me true, my jewel,
Which is he whom Ljubović has chosen?"

Softly whispered back to her the bridesman,
" Lovely maiden, beautiful Hajkuna,
Right and left I pray thee look around thee !
Do you see the old man in the distance?
Him that stately sits, like an effendi ;
Him that sits upon the crimson cushion,
With the white beard hanging to the girdle?
Mustaf-Aga, with the beard of silver—
He it is whom Ljubović has chosen."

Right and left the maiden looked around her,
Sighing deeply she beheld the bridegroom ;
And again she whispered to the bridesman,—
" Who is he that rears aloft the banner,
Riding yonder on the snowy charger,
Curly-bearded, blacker than the raven?"
Softly whispered back again the bridesman,—
" Young and noble Zuko of Udbinja,
He that sorely struggled with thy brother
In the hour when Mustaf-Aga won thee."

When the beautiful Hajkuna heard this,
Swift she dropped as if a dart had pierced her ;
Deeply sighing sank down from her saddle.
All came round to lift the lovely maiden,
Mustaf-Aga came himself to raise her ;
But she lay as if her blood were frozen
Until Zuko came. He dropped his banner,
Stretching out his hand he seized Hajkuna.
Swiftly leaped she on his horse behind him ;

Swiftly Zuko galloped for the wood-land,
Swifter raced across the plain his charger
Than a shooting star across the heavens.

Mustaf-Aga screamed unto his kindred,
" Noble guests I've asked unto my wedding,—
Ha ! the robber seizes on my maiden !
Not a hand is lifted to avenge me !"

" Aga, Aga," answered all the kindred,
" Welcome be the wild hawk to his pigeon,
It was written she should be his booty;
White and stately is thy Castle-Novo,—
There repose thee, with thy beard of silver—
Not for thee a maiden like Hajkuna."

THE DEATH OF IVO

And Ivo's aged mother had a dream :
That utter darkness settled over Senje;
The vaults of Heaven crumbled, and collapsing,
Brought down the moon upon the church of Senje;
The stars, the farthest even, fled together,
Only the morning star, a lonely watcher
In ghastly bloody garb, remained and listened;
And on the ruins of the church of Senje
A cuckoo wailed, as for her mate departed.

When she at last arose, a frightened woman,
In her right hand she took a staff, and trembling,
Went to the white-hued church to see Nedjeljko,
And told him all the horrors of her vision.
The priest, when he had heard the gloomy story,

Considered what it meant, and said, explaining:
"Your dream was bad, O mother, boding evil!
You dreamt of utter darkness over Senje?
That means, you will be lonely and forsaken.
The vaults of heaven crumbled, and collapsing,
Brought down the moon upon the church of Senje?
A cruel sudden death will come to Ivo.
The stars, even the farthest, fled together?
Poor widows many will bewail their guardian.
Only the morning star, a lonely watcher
In ghastly bloody garb, remained and listened?
With tears you shall behold your Ivo's body.
And on the ruins of the church of Senje
A cuckoo wailed, as for her mate departed?
The savage Turks will utterly destroy it,
And murder me, the agèd priest of God."
The priest had hardly finished with the omen,
When they beheld the hero doomed approaching;
The charger with the rider's blood bespattered,
Whose grievous wounds were seventeen in number.
And in the hero's left hand was the right one,
Which from its arm a keen-edged sword had
    severed.
In silence Ivo rode before his mother,
Close by the portals of the church of Senje;
And said, "O Mother! help me from my charger!
Give me a glass of wine, for I am thirsty!"
At once the mother helped him from his charger,
She gave him wine, both cooling and refreshing;
With cooling water bathed his fevered forehead.
And asked, "Has Italy been cruel to you?"
The wounded hero sighed and answered gently,
"In Italy I fared quite well, my mother;

I captured many foes and took much booty;
Unharmed I was returning to our country.
But at the very first place where we halted,
When night was setting in and we were sleepy,
Pursuers overtook us, black as ravens;
Their horses black, their mantles black as sable.
We raised our rifles once, exchanging bullets,
And not a single foe was left to fight us;
They all were killed, and none of us were wounded.
But on the second evening when we halted,
As night was setting in and we were sleepy,
Pursuers overtook us, white like marble;
Their horses white, their mantles white as ermine.
We raised our rifles once, exchanging bullets,
And not a single foe was left to fight us.
They all were killed and none of us were wounded.
But on the third night, when again we rested,
Pursuers overtook us, black as Araps;*
They brandished mighty rifles; and their garments,
As red as Eastern corals, flamed around them.
We raised our rifles once, exchanging bullets,
And then we drew our swords and fought like lions;
But not a single foe our swords have slaughtered.
My friends were killed, the only man surviving,
Your Ivo, mother, wounded, now is—dying!" . . .

Thus in his mother's arms died noble Ivo.
God grant his soul a joyous life hereafter;
To us the joy of health and cheerful hearts!

* Arap = Ethiopian, Moor.

FOLK SONGS

JAKŠIĆ DMITAR AND JAKŠIĆ BOGDANÈ

Hark! the moon is angry with the day-star:
"Tell me, day-star, where hast thou been lingering;
Three white-winged days thou art belated."
To the moon, anon, the day-star answered:
"I have wandered, moon! and I have lingered,
Over Biograd's white-hued towers; witnessed
Wonderful events. There were two brothers
Jakšić Dmitar and Jakšić Bogdanè.
They had lived harmoniously together,
Well divided all their father left them:
Dmitar took Wallachia for his portion,
Took Wallachia and entire Moldavia,
Banat also to the river Danube.
Bogdan took the level plains of Sirmia,
And the even country of the Sava;
Serbia too, up to Užice's fortress.
Dmitar's choice was this: The lower fortress
And Nebojša's tower on the Danube;
Bogdan's choice was this: The upper fortress
Within which you find the church Ružica.
Then a strife arose about a trifle—
Such a trifle; but a feud soon followed,—
A black courser and a grey-wing'd falcon!
Dmitar claims the steed, as elder brother,
Claims the steed, and claims the grey-wing'd falcon.
Bogdan will not yield or horse or falcon.

When the morning of the morrow wakened,
Dmitar, on his hand the grey-wing'd falcon,
Setting out upon his sable courser,
Rode to hunt within the mountain-forest;

And he called his wife, fair Andjelija :
" Andjelija, thou my faithful lady !
Kill with poison thou my brother Bogdan;
But if thou refuse to kill my brother,
Stay no longer in my white-hued homestead !"

When the lady heard her lord's commandment,
Down she sat all sorrowful and gloomy;
Carefully she thought the matter over,
" What am I to do ? Poor wretched woman !
Shall I kill my brother—kill with poison !—
If I kill my cruel husband's brother
'Twere a monstrous crime before high heaven,
'Twere a sin and shame before my people.
Great and small would point their fingers at me,
Saying—' That is the unhappy woman
Who has killed her cruel husband's brother !'
But if I refuse to poison Bogdan,
Never shall I see again my husband !"

Thus she mused until a thought relieved her;
She descended to the castle's cavern,
Took the consecrated cup of blessing
Made of purest gold, her father's present
Given to her when she married Dmitar;
Full of golden wine she filled the vessel,
And she bore it to her brother Bogdan.
Low to earth she bowed herself before him,
And she kissed his hands and garments meekly.
" Take this consecrated cup of blessing
Made of purest gold, my father's present
Which he gave me when I married Dmitar,
Filled with golden wine by me, my brother.

Give me for my cup a horse and falcon."
Bogdan, deeply moved, heard her entreaty,
Willingly he gave her horse and falcon.

Meanwhile Dmitar in the mountain-forest
Without finding anything, was hunting
All day long, when with the fall of evening
He chanced upon a lake of greenish colour,
Where a golden-pinion'd duck was swimming.
Dmitar then released his grey-wing'd falcon,
Bade him seize the golden-pinion'd swimmer.
Faster than the hunter's eye could follow,
Lo! the duck had seized the grey-wing'd falcon,
Leaving then his foe with one wing broken.
Dmitar, when he saw his bird's misfortune
Stripped and plunged at once and fetched the falcon;
Soothing his belovéd fellow-hunter
With compassionate words: " My faithful falcon,
Tell me what it feels like to be suffering?"

Hissing, said the falcon to his master:
" With a broken wing I feel disheartened,
Saddened as if I had lost a brother."
Dmitar was uneasy. He remembered
That his wife was charged to kill his brother.
Lightning-like he leaped into the saddle,
Racing with his horse to Biograd's fortress,
Praying that his brother had not perished.
Thundering across the bridge of Čekmek,
Dmitar spurred his raven steed so fiercely,
That the courser rushing like a whirlwind
Crashing through the flooring broke his fore-legs.

Dmitar took the saddle off his courser,
Flung it on his heavy grievous cudgel
And ran on alone to Biograd's fortress

There, he sent at once for Andjelija,
"Tell me, faithful Andjelija, tell me,
Hast thou killed my brother as I bade thee?"
Sweet indeed was Andjelija's answer:
"No, indeed, I have not killed thy brother;
I have reconciled thee to thy brother."

MARKO'S FALCON

Vezir Murat is gone out a-hunting,
Hunting in the leafy mountain-forest:
With him hunt twelve warriors, Turkish heroes:
With the heroes hunts the noble Marko;
White days three they hunted in the mountain;
Nothing found they in the mountain-forest.
But, behold! while in the forest hunting,
Chance has led them to a green-faced water,
Where a flock of gold-wing'd ducks are swimming.

There the proud Vezir lets loose his falcon,
Bids him pounce upon a gold-wing'd swimmer;
Easily the duck escaped the danger,
Vanishing within the clouds of heaven.
To the proud Vezir, said princely Marko,
"Vezir Murat! will it be allowed me
To let loose my own, my favourite falcon
To bring down the gold-wing'd duck from heaven?"
And the mighty Moslem answered Marko:

"Certainly I give permission. Do so!"
Then the princely Marko loosed his falcon;
To the clouds of heaven aloft he mounted;
Then he pounced upon the gold-wing'd swimmer—
Seized him—rose—and down they fell together.
When the Vezir's bird beheld the struggle,
He became indignant with vexation:
'Twas of old his custom to play falsely,
And appropriate the bag of others.
So he set upon his finer rival
To deprive him of his well-earn'd trophy.
But the bird was valiant as his master,
Marko's falcon had the mind of Marko:
And his gold-wing'd prey he would not yield him.
Sharply he attacked the Vezir's falcon,
And he tore away his finest feathers.

Soon as the Vezir observed the contest,
He was filled with sorrow and with anger;
Rushed upon the falcon of Prince Marko,
Dashed him fiercely 'gainst a verdant fir-tree,
And he broke the falcon's dexter pinion.
Marko's noble falcon groaned in suffering,
As the serpent hisses from the cavern.
Marko flew to help his favourite falcon,
Bound with tenderness the wounded pinion,
And enraged, he thus addressed his favourite:
" Woe to me, and woe to thee, my falcon!
We have left the Serbians—we have hunted
With the Turks,—and suffered thus injustice."

Then the hunting party started quickly,
Passed him by, and left him sad and lonely.

Marko tarried in the mountain-forests,
Carefully to dress the wounded falcon.
After that he leaped into the saddle
Spurred his steed and sped across the woodland.
Šarac swifter than the mountain Vila
Quickly took his lord and master Marko
To the borders of the gloomy forest.
On the plain beneath him halts the Vezir
And the hunting-party, heroes twelve.
Amurath descries the princely Marko,
And thus calls upon his twelve companions:—
" Ye, my children ! ye, twelve Turkish heroes !
See ye yonder mountain-mist approaching,
From the darksome mountain travelling hither?
In that mountain-mist is princely Marko ;
Lo ! how fiercely urges he his courser !
Heaven knows ! this business will end badly !"
Soon the princely Marko reached the Moslems,
From the sheath he drew his trusty sabre,
Drove before him all the Turkish heroes,
As the vulture drives a flock of sparrows.
Soon he overtook the flying warriors,
From his neck their chieftain's head he severed ;
And the dozen youths his trusty sabre
Into four-and-twenty halves divided.

Then he stood a while in doubtful musing :
Should he go to Jedren to the Sultan—
Should he rather seek his home at Prilip?
And at last he came to this decision :
" Better I myself inform the Sultan,
And let Marko tell the deeds of Marko—
Not the foes of Marko,—not the Moslems !"

When the hero Marko came to Jedren,
To the Sultan in Divan he entered.
Marko's eyes were rolling, blazing fiercely
Like a wolf's, who, hungry, roams the forest,
Flashing from beneath his brows like lightning.
And the Sultan asked the hero Marko,
" Tell me what hath vexed thee, princely Marko?
Say in what the Sultan has annoyed thee?
Tell me, as your friend, of your misfortune."
Then the princely Marko told the Sultan
What had happened to the hunting-party.
And the Sultan roared with laughter, saying :
" Blessings be upon thee, noble Marko !
Hadst thou acted otherwise, my Marko,
Son of mine I would no longer call thee.
Any Turk may get a Vezir's title,
But there is no hero like my Marko."

From his silken raiment then the Sultan
Drew his purse and took a thousand ducats,
Threw the golden ducats to the hero :
" Take these ducats from thy master, Marko,
Drink my health, thou bravest of all heroes !"

Marko took the purse of gold in silence,
Walked away in silence from the Divan ;
'Twas no love for Marko,—no intention
That the hero's lips should pledge the Sultan :
'Twas that he should quickly quit the monarch,
For his fearful wrath had been awakened.

MARKO AND THE MOORISH MAIDEN

Once the mother of the princely Marko
Thus addressed her son: " Now, Marko, tell me
Why hast thou so many a shrine erected?
Is it for thy sins in lowly penance?
Is it that thy wealth is overflowing?"

Then the noble prince addressed his mother:
" Now by Heav'n I'll tell thee! Once I travelled
Through the distant realms of black-skinned Araps:
One day early I went to a cistern
To refresh my Šarac:—round the cistern
Were a dozen Moorish men assembled.
Through the Moors I fain would reach the water
That my Šarac should not tire from waiting.
But the dozen Moorish men opposed me,
We began to fight about it fiercely,
And my trusty club aloft I lifted:
One of the black Moors I soon had finished,
One I struck to earth,—eleven assailed me:
Two I struck to earth,—and ten attacked me:
Three I struck to earth,—and nine engaged me:
Four I struck to earth,—and twice four smote me:
Five I struck to earth,—and strove with seven:
Six I struck to earth,—and faced as many:
But the six became my masters, bound me,
Led me swiftly to the Moorish palace,
And their monarch sentenced me to prison.

Seven long years I dwelt within my dungeon:
Nothing knew I of the summer's coming;
Nothing knew I of returning winter;

Two things only told me of the seasons;
Snow was sometimes thrown into my prison
By the maidens snowballing each other :
Then I knew it was the winter season.
Sometimes maidens threw me basil-nosegays,
Then I knew it was the dawn of summer.
When the eighth year broke upon thy Marko,
It was not the dungeon that distressed him,
The tormentor was a Moorish maiden,
And she was the Moorish monarch's daughter.
Every day at morning and at evening
She came calling to my dungeon-window,
' Nay ! thou shalt not perish in thy prison,
Thou poor Marko ! give me but thy promise
That thou wilt espouse the Moorish maiden,
If the maiden will unlock thy prison—
If she will release thy faithful Šarac,
I will bring a heap of golden ducats :
All the ducats thou canst wish for, Marko.'

When I heard her in my misery, mother,
From my head I took my cap, and laid it
On my knees,—and on the cap I swore her,
' By my faith ! I'll never leave thee, maiden !
By my faith ! I never will betray thee !
Even the golden sun is sometimes fickle—
Shines not out in winter as in summer;
But my faith, my word, shall be unchanging !'
And the maiden trusted Marko's promise,
She believed the oath that I had sworn her ;
She unlocked the portals of my dungeon :
From my prison-house she led me, mother,
Led me to my proud and prancing Šarac :

For herself she brought a steed still nobler:
Both were loaded well with bags of ducats:
And she brought my bright and faithful sabre.
On our steeds we sprang, and swiftly journeyed
In the darkness, from the Moorish country.
But at last the morning dawned upon us,
We dismounted and sat down to slumber,
And she threw her swarthy arms around me.
But as daylight came, and I,—O mother!—
When I saw how black her face—O mother!—
When I saw her teeth as white as ivory,
Such a fright and such a shuddering seized me,
That I drew the sabre from its scabbard,
Plunged it deeply through her silken girdle;
Through and through the keen-edged sabre smote
  her.
Then I leaped upon the back of Šarac,
And I heard the maiden's lips still murmur,
' Thou in God my brother! thou, O Marko,
Leave me not! thou wretch, O do not leave me!'

Therefore, mother! do I lowly penance:
Thus, my mother, have I gold o'erflowing:
Therefore found I charities abundant:
Therefore have I many a shrine erected."

THE DEATH OF MARKO

At the dawn of day the noble Marko
Rode in sunlight on a Sabbath morning;
By the sea, into the Urvinian mountains;
But when he the mountains had ascended,
Suddenly his trusty Šarac stumbled;
Šarac stumbled, and began to weep there.
Sad it fell upon the heart of Marko,
And he thus addressed his favourite Šarac,
" Ah ! my faithful friend, my trusty Šarac,
Brother in arms ! A hundred years and sixty
We have been together as companions,
And till now my Šarac never stumbled.
Thou hast stumbled now, my trusty Šarac,
Thou hast stumbled, and thine eyes are weeping.
God alone can tell what fate awaits me;—
One of us is surely doomed to perish,
And my life or thine is now in peril."

While he thus addressed his faithful Šarac,
Lo ! the Vila from Urvina's mountain
Called aloud unto the princely Marko :
" Brother, listen—listen, princely Marko !
Know'st thou why thy faithful Šarac stumbled?
Know that he was mourning for his master;
Know, his heart forebodes ye will be parted."
Marko answered thus the mountain Vila :
" Thou white Vila, let a curse be on thee !
How can I be parted from my Šarac,
Who, through many a land and town hath borne me,
From the sun's uprising to his setting.

Better steed ne'er trod the earth than Šarac,
As than Marko never better hero.
While my head rests firmly on my shoulders,
Never will I from my steed be severed."

The white Vila answered princely Marko:
"Brother, listen—listen, princely Marko!
Force will never tear thy Šarac from thee;
Club nor battling-lance nor keen-edged sabre
Wielded by a giant's arm could kill thee.
Earth no hero holds who can alarm thee:—
But the brave must die—and thou art mortal;
God will smite thee—God, the old blood-shedder.
But if thou would'st doubt the mountain-Vila,
Hasten to the summit of the mountain
Look to right and look to left around thee:
Thou wilt see two tall and slender fir-trees,
Tall enough to overlook the forest;
Covered are these trees with verdant needles,
And between the fir-trees is a fountain.
Look! and afterwards rein back thy Šarac,
Then alight and bind him to the fir-tree:
Bend thee down,—and look into the fountain;
Look,—as if the fountain were a mirror;
Look, and thou shalt see when death awaits thee."

Marko did, as counselled by the Vila.
When he came upon the mountain summit,
To the right and left he looked around him;
Then he saw two tall and slender fir-trees,
Tall enough to overlook the forest,
Covered with a wealth of verdant needles.
Then he reined his faithful Šarac backwards,

Then dismounted, tied him to the fir-tree;
And bent down, and looked into the fountain,
Saw his face upon the water mirror'd,
Saw his death-day written on the water.

Tears were trickling down the cheeks of Marko,
"O, thou faithless world!—thou lovely flower!
Thou wert lovely—a short pilgrim's journey—
Short—though I have seen three centuries over—
And 'tis time that I should end my journey!"

Then he drew his sharp and shining sabre,
Drew it forth—and loosed the sabre-girdle;
And he hastened to his faithful Šarac:
With one stroke he cleft his head asunder,
That he never should by Turk be mounted,
Never be disgraced in Turkish service,
Water draw, or drag a Moslem's djugum.*
Marko, when he had beheaded Šarac,
Made a grave to bury his companion,
Nobler grave than that which held his brother!
Then he broke in four his trusty sabre,
That it might not be a Moslem's portion,
That it might not be the boast of Moslems,
And the Christians' curse should follow Marko.
Next he broke his trusty lance in seven;
Threw the fragments to the fir-trees' branches.
Then he took his club, so terror-striking,
In his powerful right hand, and flung it,
Flung it from the mountain of Urvina,
Far into the azure, gloomy ocean.

* Djugum = a large copper cauldron.

To his club thus spoke the hero Marko:
" When my club returneth from the ocean,
Shall a hero come to equal Marko."

When he thus had broken all his weapons,
From his belt he drew a golden pencil,
From his pocket snow-white writing paper,
And the princely Marko wrote upon it,
" He who visits the Urvina mountain,
He who seeks the fountain by the fir-trees,
And there finds the hero Marko's body,
Let him know that Marko is departed.
On him are three purses filled with ducats;
One shall be his portion, with my blessing,
Who shall dig a grave for Marko's body:
Let the second be the Church's portion;
Let the third be given to blind and crippled,
That the blind on earth in peace may wander,
And with hymns laud Marko's deeds of glory."

Now when Marko had inscribed the letter,
Lo! he stuck it on the fir-tree's branches,
That it might be seen by passing travellers;
Threw his golden pen into the fountain;
Doff'd his vest of green, and spread it calmly
On the grass, beneath a sheltering fir-tree;
Cross'd himself, and lay down on his garment.
O'er his eyes he drew his cap of sable,
Thus the hero fell asleep for ever.

By the fountain lay the lifeless Marko,
Day and night, a whole long week he rested.
Many travellers passed, and saw the hero,—

FOLK SONGS

Saw him lying near the public high-way;
And while passing said, " The hero slumbers!"
Then they kept a more than common distance,
Fearing that they might disturb the hero.

Fortune oft is followed by misfortune,
As Misfortune oft is Fortune's leader.
'Twas good fortune then, that Abbot Basil
Coming from the white church Vilindara,*
With his scholar, with the young Isaije,
Thither came, and saw the sleeping Marko.
Pointing to the hero, said the Abbot:
" O, my son, be cautious, lest thou wake him!
He is out of humour when awakening,
And without remorse he might destroy us."
Looking anxiously around him, Basil
Saw the letter on the fir-tree branches;
Read it from a distance;—and he trembled,
Read that Marko had this life departed.
From his horse the frightened monk alighted,
Seized the hand of Marko;—Marko moved not!
Long he had been dead,—long since departed!

Tears rushed swiftly from the eyes of Basil,
Marko's fate filled all his heart with sorrow.
From the girdle then he took the purses,
Which he hid within his own white girdle:
In his mind the Abbot was resolving
Where he should entomb the hero Marko.
Thinking hard, the monk at last decided;
On his horse he placed the hero's body,

* Vilindara = Chilendar.

Took it down the mountains to the sea-shore,
Thence he shipped it to the Holy Mountain,
Landing near the white church, Vilindara,
To that white church he conveyed the body;
And, as wont, above the hero's body
Funeral hymns were sung; and he was buried
In the white church aisle, the very centre,—
But no monument was raised above him,
Lest his foes should find the hero's grave-stone,
And in their malignant joy destroy it.

THE FALL OF THE SERBIAN EMPIRE

From Jerusalem, the Holy City,
Lo! there flew a grey and royal falcon;
Carrying in his claws a little swallow.
No! it was no gray and royal falcon,
'Twas Elias! 'twas the holy prophet;
And he did not bring a little swallow,
But a letter from God's holy mother
To the Tsar upon the Field of Blackbirds.
At the Emperor's feet he dropped the letter,
And the missive thus addressed the Emperor:

"Tsar Lazar! thou Tsar of noble lineage!
Tell me now, what kingdom art thou choosing?
Wilt thou choose the kingdom of hereafter?
Or dost thou prefer an earthly kingdom?
Wouldst thou rather rule an earthly kingdom,
Saddle thy good steed,—and gird him tightly;
Let thy heroes buckle on their sabres,
Smite the Turkish legions like a tempest,

And these legions all will fly before thee.
But if thou preferr'st the realms of Heaven,
Pitch a tent upon the Field of Blackbirds,
Wrought of silk and scarlet. Consecrate it
To a house of God and let your army
Enter and receive the Holy Supper,
To become a host of white-souled warriors
Ready for that end which is their portion:
For thy warriors all are doomed to perish;
Thou, too, Prince, shalt perish with thy army."

When the Tsar Lazar had read the writing,
Many were his thoughts and long his musings.
"Lord, my God! what—which shall be my
 portion,
Which my choice of these two proffer'd kingdoms?
Shall I choose God's kingdom? Shall I rather
Choose an earthly one? For what is earthly
Is all fleeting, vain, and unsubstantial;
Heavenly things are lasting, firm, eternal."

So the Tsar preferred a heavenly kingdom
Rather than an earthly. On Kosovo
He erects a church, wrought not of marble
But of purest silk and deepest scarlet.
Then he calls the Patriarch of Serbia,
Calls around him all the twelve Archbishops,
Bids them make the Holy Supper ready,
Purify the warriors from their errors,
And for death's encounter make them ready.

Thus the warriors were prepared for battle,
And the Turkish hosts approached Kosovo.

Bogdan leads his valiant heroes forward,
With his sons—all grim and fearless fighters,
Sharp and keen—nine grey and noble falcons,
Each the leader of nine thousand warriors,
And the aged Jug led twenty thousand.

Now began the fierce and bloody battle.
Seven Pashas, overcome, were scattered,
But the eighth came pressing boldly onwards.
Then the aged Bogdan and his offspring—
Nine grey noble falcons—fell together!
With them fell their hosts of valiant warriors.

Now advance Mrnjavčević's warriors,
Ban* Uglješa's and Vojvoda† Gojko's;
Vukašin a king and warrior with them.
Each one leads full thirty thousand warriors.
Now begins the fierce and bloody battle;
Pashas eight are overcome and scattered,
But the ninth is pressing boldly onwards,
And he slays the two Mrnjavčević
Ban Uglješa and Vojvoda Gojko,
Vukašin the king and warrior with them;
They are trodden down by Turkish horses,
And the warriors perish with their leaders.

Now the ducal Stevan presses forward:
Strong and mighty is the ducal army,
Numbering sixty thousand valiant warriors,
And the battle with the Turks commences.

* Ban = lord.
† Vojvoda = duke.

Pashas nine are overcome and scattered,
But the tenth came rushing boldly onwards;
And the ducal Stevan is defeated,
And his warriors perish with their leader.

Then Lazar, the noble lord of Serbia
Seeks Kosovo with his mighty army;
Seven and seventy thousand Serbian warriors!
How the infidels retire before him,
And they dare not face his awful anger.
Now indeed begins the glorious battle;
And he would have crushed the Turkish forces,
But for Vuk,—the curse of God be on him!
Who betrayed his kinsman at Kosovo.—
Thus the Turkish army was victorious,
Thus the hero fell, the Tsar of Serbia.—
But they have been honoured, and are holy,
In the keeping of the God of heaven.

KOSOVO

That night came two black ravens
      from Kosovo field,
And round about the tower
      in the red dawn they wheeled;
Round it and round it
      with many a croak they flew,
When they perched upon the turret
      more loud their croaking grew.
Ho! is this the castle
      of that famous king?
It is a silent castle—
      it holds no living thing.

The solitary lady
>   heard them where she lay,
Up went she to the turret,
>   in the dawning grey;
"Ye two black ravens,
>   God greet ye well this hour,
Why come ye here so early,
>   to croak about the tower?
Over Kosovo field
>   was it your luck to fly?—
Saw ye two mighty hosts
>   that thereupon did lie?
Saw ye the meeting, ravens?—
>   did ye hear the din?—
Tell me the truth, black ravens,
>   which of them did win?"

"Fair thanks for such greeting,"
>   said the ravens black,
"We have been to Kosovo,
>   We are just come back;
Two mighty hosts, fair lady,
>   It was our luck to see,
Yesterday they fought,
>   and near enough were we;
The princes of the armies
>   are slaughtered, both the two,
And all the Turks are dead
>   except a very few;
Some of the Serbian warriors
>   still remain in life,
But every breast among them
>   is gashed with lance or knife."

While the black birds were croaking
   in Milica's ear,
Her servant Milutin,
   a faithful man, drew near;
His right hand, parted from the wrist,
   in the left he bore—
Down his horse's side
   the streams of blood did pour;
Seventeen wounds, I ween,
   Milutin's blood did drain
Ere he turned his horse's head
   from Kosovo plain.
" What's that?—poor Milutin ! "
   ('twas thus the lady said)
" Speak, was there any treason,
   that the Tsar is dead?"

Milutin, the servant,
   his lady thus did greet :—
" Help me quickly, lady,
   help me from my seat;
Bring cold water from the well,
   and wash my burning brow,
And pour me wine, red wine,
   for I have thirst, I trow,
I am sorely wounded,
   my heart is bloodless now."

The beautiful Milica
   helped him from his steed,
And she washed his brows
   glowing like a gleed;
She filled the cup with wine,
   and held it to his head,

And when some strength was come,
   it was thus she said,
" Now, Milutin, look up,
   and all thy tidings yield,
Tell me how it went
   upon Kosovo field;
First, of the famous prince,
   how he was slaughtered tell,
And my father, Jug Bogdanè,
   where the old man fell,
And my noble brothers,
   all the noble nine,
And Miloš the vojvoda,
   that dear friend of mine,
And Vuk, the fearless lord,
   the leader of the clan,
And young and bold Strahinja,
   the son of the old Ban?"

The soldier raised his head,
   and thus his tale begun,—
" They lie upon Kosovo,
   slaughtered every one;
Where the famous prince,
   the Tsar, my master, lies,
Has blood enow been shed,
   all the grass it dyes;
With lances broke and shivered
   is the ground bestrewn,
Many a Turkish lance,
   but more of them our own;
For the Serbian soldiers
   clustered from afar

To defend their master,
        and died about the Tsar.
For your father, Jug Bogdanè,
        I saw the good old man
Struck down among the foremost,
        as the fight began;
Eight of your gallant brothers
        were slaughtered by his side,
The band stuck fast together
        till all but one had died;
It was Boško Jugović,
        he alone was left—
I saw him raise his banner,
        as out his way he cleft;
In like an eagle then
        among the Turks went he,
And scattered them like doves
        till the blood was at his knee.

Strahinja sleeps, and Miloš,
        an everlasting sleep,
In Sitnica's waters,
        in the waters cold and deep.
But ere Miloš was slain,
        the Lord had blessed his hand
To do a deed of glory
        for the Serbian land,—
With his own hand he slew
        the Sultan Amurath!
God bless his soul for that,
        and all the kin he hath!
O sung in many a song,
        and told in many a tale,

While green Kosovo lasts,
        his memory shall not fail.
Why did you ask for Vuk?
        A curse upon his soul!
A curse upon his mother,
        his house, his children's scroll!
He in that hour went over
        to the heathen host,
He and his false twelve thousand;
        and thus the Tsar was lost."

FAIRY-TALES

" The Language of these fairy-tales is everywhere simple and natural."
J. G<small>RIMM</small>

WHY THE SOLE OF MAN'S FOOT IS FLAT

Once upon a time, when the devils turned recreants to God and fled to earth, amongst other things, they took along with them the Sun, which the Tsar of the devils stuck on the point of his lance and he carried it over his shoulder. But when the Earth complained to God that she would soon be burnt to ashes by the Sun, God sent the Holy Archangel Michael to try by some means or other to take away the Sun from the devil. Now, when the Holy Archangel stepped down to the earth he made friends with the Tsar of the devils, but the latter saw at once what was Michael's little game, and was always on his guard.

One day the two went together for a walk, and went on and on until they came to the sea. There they made preparations to have a bathe, and the devil stuck his lance into the ground with the Sun still upon it. After they had been bathing for a while, the Holy Archangel said:—" Now, let us dive and see who can dive deepest." And the devil said, " Very well !" So the Holy Archangel dived first, and brought up in his mouth some sand from the bottom of the sea. Now it was the devil's turn to dive, but he was afraid that Michael would steal the Sun. Then he had a fine idea : he spit on the ground, and out of his spittle grew a magpie. He told her to look after the Sun whilst he was diving to get some sand from the bottom of the sea. As soon, however, as the devil dived, the Holy Archangel made the sign of the cross, and instantly the sea was covered with ice nine yards thick. Quickly he seized the Sun, spread out his wings, and flew heavenwards, whilst the magpie croaked for all she was worth. When the devil heard the magpie's voice he guessed at once what was the matter, and returned as quickly as possible. But when he came near the surface he found that the sea was frozen up and that he could not get out. Hurriedly he made again for the bottom of the sea, fetched a stone, broke through the ice, and pressed on in pursuit of the Holy Archangel. The distance between the two grew less and less. Now the Angel had reached the Gate of Heaven and had already put one foot inside, when the devil just caught him by the other foot and tore out of it a large piece of flesh with his claws. And as the Holy Archangel with the regained Sun in his hands stepped before God, he wept and lamented," What shall I do now disfigured thus?" Then the Lord God said to him, " Be still and fear not; henceforth shall all men bear a small hollow in the sole of the foot." And as God had said, so it came about that all men received a small hollow in the sole of each foot.

THE RAM WITH THE GOLDEN FLEECE

Once upon a time a huntsman went to hunt in the mountains. Quite suddenly he saw a ram coming towards him, and its wool was of the purest gold. As soon as the huntsman beheld it he took aim with his rifle to kill the ram, but before he could fire the beast rushed at him and pierced him with its horns, so that he fell dead. Afterwards his companions found him, and did not know who had murdered him, but they carried him home and buried him.

The huntsman's wife, however, took the rifle and hung it up on a nail. When her son had grown up to a vigorous youth he demanded the rifle from his mother in order to go a-hunting with it. But the mother would not consent. "Not for anything in the world will I give you this rifle, for through it your father perished; and now you will risk your life too?" One day, however, the lad took the rifle without his mother's knowledge and went a-hunting.

When he entered the wood, suddenly the ram crossed his path and said, "I have killed your father, and now I shall kill you." The youth was terribly frightened, but he said, "God! help me!" took aim, and killed the ram.

Now, the lad was of course very pleased to have killed a ram with a golden fleece, for there was not another like it in the whole of the land. He skinned the ram, and carried the fleece home.

By and by the report of his deed reached the Tsar's ears, and the latter commanded that the fleece should be shown to him, because he wanted to know all the wild animals of his forests. When the youth had brought the fleece, the Tsar said, "Tell me what you want for the fleece." But he would not sell it at any price.

Now the Tsar had a minister who was the youth's cousin and bore him a grudge. He said to the Tsar, "If the fellow does not want to give you the fleece let us try to get rid of him. Ask him, therefore, to do something that is impossible." And in this way he enticed the Tsar, who finally called the youth back and told him that he was to plant a vineyard from which new wine could be had within seven days.

When the youth heard this order he began to weep and to implore the Tsar not to demand impossibilities, but the Tsar was firm and said, " If within seven days you have not done what I ask, you will lose your head." Then the youth went home weeping and told his mother what had happened, but she said, " Did I not tell you, my son, that that rifle would cost you your life just as it cost your father's?"

Disheartened, the youth left the village, reflecting all the time what he was to do and how he might escape death. He had gone quite a long way when he suddenly beheld a beautiful maiden by his side. She asked him, " Why do you weep, my brother?" But he answered crossly, " For God's sake, go away; you cannot help me!" And he continued on his way. The young girl, however, followed him, and urged him to confide in her. " Perhaps," she said, " I may be able to help you after all." At last he yielded, and said, " Very well, I'll tell you, although I know that no one but God can help me." And he told her everything.

When he had finished his story, she said, " Be of good cheer, my brother, and not afraid! Go to the Tsar and ask him in what place the vineyard is to be situated, and demand that it is to be marked out for you; then take a knapsack, put into it a small sprig of basil, go to the place pointed out by him and lie down to sleep, and after seven days you shall have ripe grapes." Then he returned home and told his mother what he had heard, and she said, " Go, go, by all means, since it cannot make things worse." Thereupon he proceeded to the Tsar, asked for an allotment for his vineyard, and that the furrows might be ploughed for him. The Tsar granted all he asked. Then the youth took upon his shoulders a knapsack, put into it a small branch of basil, went to the place appointed, and in a sad mood he went to sleep. When he awoke the first morning the vines were planted; the next day they were growing lustily; and after seven days the grapes were ripe, and this at a time of the year when there were none to be had anywhere else. He gathered them, pressed them, and brought to the Tsar sweet wine, and in a cloth fresh grapes.

When the Tsar saw them he was much astonished, and everybody in the castle was amazed. Then the wicked cousin of the youth spoke again to the Tsar, and said, " This time we will set him a task so hard that he cannot possibly execute it." Thus influenced by evil counsel, the Tsar again called for the youth and said, " Now you shall build me a castle of ivory !"

When the youth heard this he went weeping to his mother and told her about the Tsar's new command. " That," he said," is absolutely impossible; I shall never be able to do it." The mother, however, replied, " My son, go again out of the village; perhaps God is kind enough to let you meet that girl once more." And again he left the village, and again at the same spot where he had met her before he saw the maiden, who said, "My brother, why are you again so sad and tearful?" Then he told her about the impossible task imposed on him. When the girl had listened to the end of his words, she said, "That shall be quite an easy matter for you. Go, and ask the Tsar for a ship, for three hundred barrels of wine, and three hundred kegs of brandy, and finally for twelve carpenters. Then go on board ship, and when you arrive between two mountain-chains, drain off the water which you will find there and pour in its stead wine and brandy into the river-bed. When the elephants come to drink water they will become intoxicated and fall down one after another. Then the carpenters must quickly saw off the elephants' tusks. Carry these to the place where the Tsar wants the castle to be built. There lie down and go to sleep without any further care. In seven days the castle shall be ready."

Thereupon the youth returned home and told his mother about all this, and she said, "Go, my dear son, perhaps God will help you again this time." Then he went to the Tsar, asked for everything he wanted, and when he had obtained his wine, his brandy, and his carpenters he did exactly what he had been told. And the elephants really did come; they got drunk; the carpenters sawed off their tusks and carried them to the place where the castle was to be built. The young man, however, one evening took a tiny branch of basil in his knapsack, went also to that place, and lay down to sleep, and after seven days the castle was ready.

When the Tsar saw the finished castle he was amazed, and he said to his minister, the youth's cousin, " What are we to do with that fellow? He is not an ordinary human being; the gods know what he is." And the minister replied, " One more thing you should order him to do, and if he achieves that too, then indeed he is a supernatural being." And thus he persuaded the Tsar to call the youth once more, and he said to him, " Now you shall bring me the Imperial Princess, the daughter of our neighbour, the Emperor! Should you fail to bring her, you will lose your life."

When the youth had heard this, he again went to his mother and told her what the Tsar had ordered, and she advised him, " Go, my dear son, and look again for that wise and beautiful maiden. Perhaps God will grant that she may deliver you also this time." And he went out of the village, found the maiden, and told her about his task. The maiden calmly listened, and said, " First go and ask from the Tsar a big ship, and in the ship fit out twelve booths, put the most lovely goods for sale into the booths, different goods in each one; then ask for twelve of the most handsome youths to be dressed most gorgeously, and make them salesmen in your twelve booths. When your ship has been supplied, set sail. Then when on your journey you will meet a man who carries a live eagle; ask the man whether he will sell it. He will not object, and you must give whatever price he may ask for it. After that you will meet another man in a small boat who has a carp, and the scales of this carp will be pure gold. Buy the carp, whatever the price! At last you will meet another man who is carrying a live pigeon, and also this pigeon you must buy and pay for it whatever is asked. After that take a feather from the eagle's tail, a scale from the carp, and a feather from the pigeon's left wing. Thereupon give the three animals their freedom. Now, when you have arrived in the Emperor's capital, pitch your twelve booths in front of his castle, and place one of your handsome salesmen before each booth. Then all the people in the castle will come forth to inspect your lovely wares and admire them, and the maidens that come to fetch water will tell the people in the town that as long as the town has existed never have been seen such a beautiful ship and such lovely wares. Even the Imperial Princess will hear about it, and she will appeal to her father for permission to view the goods. And when together with her playmates she comes to the booths, lead her and her party from booth to booth, and before her eyes spread the most lovely goods which you have and try to keep her interested until dark sets in. And once it gets really dark, set sail! A thick fog will fall at that moment, so that no one can see anything. The princess, however, will have a favourite little bird on her shoulder, which she has always with her, and when she notices that the ship is moving she will put the bird upon its wings to report at home in the castle what has happened. But you then must burn the eagle feather, and at once the eagle will come; bid him catch the little bird, and he will do it. Thereupon the maiden will throw a small pebble into the sea, and, lo! the ship will stand stock-still.

Then you must burn the scale from the carp, and at once the carp will come swimming along; bid the carp find and swallow the stone, and the carp will do so, whereupon the ship will move again. After you have been travelling undisturbed for a long while, at last you will arrive between two mountains. There the ship will be turned into stone quite suddenly, and you all will be very much frightened. The princess will then urge you to fetch her some Water of Life. Then you must burn the pigeon's feather, and without delay the pigeon will come; give it a small flask, and in this the pigeon will bring you some Water of Life, whereupon the ship will turn, and happily you will arrive home with the princess."

When the young man had carefully noted everything that the maiden had told him, he went home and told his mother. Then he went to the Tsar and asked for all the things necessary. The Tsar did not like to refuse, and gave him all he asked. Thereupon he set out for his voyage, and everything happened exactly as he had been told. And when the youth arrived in front of the Imperial castle he did all the maiden had bidden him, carried off the Emperor's daughter, and happily came back with her. Already from afar the Tsar and his wicked minister beheld the returning ship, and the minister said to the Tsar, " There is nothing left but to kill him the moment he leaves the ship."

When the ship had anchored, they all, one after another, left the ship, first the princess with her playmates, then the twelve young men, and finally our friend. The Tsar, however, had already posted an executioner, who, the moment he stepped on land, beheaded him. The Tsar now wanted to marry the princess himself, and he hastened towards her to kiss her. But she turned away from him and exclaimed, " Where is the youth who has taken so much trouble about me?" And when she saw that he was beheaded, quickly she took some drops from the Water of Life, sprinkled them on the youth, placed the head in its proper place, and at once he was alive again, as though nothing had happened.

Seeing this, the Tsar's wicked counsellor said, " Now he has returned from the dead he will know even more than before." And the Tsar, anxious to find it all out for himself, gave the order to be beheaded himself, and he asked the princess thereafter to revive him with the Water of Life. But when the Tsar's head was cut off the princess did not trouble about it at all. She wrote a letter to her father, in which she told him the whole story, and that she intended marrying the youth. The Emperor wrote back that the people were to recognize the youth as their Tsar; should they refuse to do so he would invade their country. The people, however, were quite willing to acknowledge him as their Tsar. And so he married the Imperial Princess and became Tsar, and the twelve young men who had accompanied him married the maidens in the retinue of the princess, and they all became great Lords, and he gave them large estates.

ABOUT THE MAIDEN SWIFTER THAN A HORSE

Once upon a time there lived a maiden. She had not been begotten by a father and a mother, but the Vile had shaped her out of snow, which they had fetched up on St. Elias' day in the height of summer from out of a bottomless pit. The wind had breathed life into the form; dew had nourished it; the forest had clothed it with leaves; and the meadow had adorned it with most beautiful flowers. She was whiter than the snow, rosier than the prettiest rose, more brilliant than the sun. She was so beautiful that there never was a girl like her, nor ever will be.

This maiden announced on a certain day that on a fixed date a race would be held in such and such a place, and that she would marry the youth who on horseback would be able to overtake her, relying on her own fleetness. Within a few days the news had spread throughout the world, and thousands of suitors at once gathered together, all mounted on the most magnificent steeds, each one appearing still more splendid than the other. Even the Tsar's son came into the race-course. The suitors all seated on horseback now took their places side by side in a row; the maiden, however, without a horse, stood in their midst and said, " There, near the goal, I have set up a golden apple. Whoever arrives there first and takes the apple may claim me as his wife. But if I reach the goal before you and get the apple, all of you will then drop dead;

so now you know the risk, therefore consider well what you are going to do."

The horsemen, however, were all infatuated; each hoped to win the maiden, and they said to one another, "We are absolutely certain that the maiden on foot cannot escape any one of us, and someone whom God and Fortune favour must and will lead her home!" Then, on the given signal, they all raced along the course. When they had covered half the distance the girl was already far ahead, for she spread out tiny wings under her shoulders. Then the horsemen swore at one another, and spurred and whipped their horses, and they were just coming close up to the maiden when she, perceiving it, pulled a hair from the top of her head and threw it away. At once a large wood arose, and the suitors lost all sense of direction. Only after some time they succeeded in tracking the maiden, who, of course, was now far ahead. But again the horsemen spurred and whipped their horses, and again overtook her. And the maiden saw herself to be in danger of defeat; she wept a tear, and the tear grew into a rapid and roaring river, in which nearly all the suitors got drowned; and only the Tsar's son, swimming with his horse through the river, pursued the maiden. And when he saw that the maiden had passed quickly ahead he threw a spell over her, mentioning the name of God and asking her to stand still. This she did. He picked her up, put her behind him on his horse, swam back through the river, and returned home through a chain of mountains; but when he had reached the highest mountain-peak and turned round, the maiden had vanished.

HONESTY IS NE'ER AN ILL PENNYWORTH

Once upon a time there was a poor man who had hired himself out to a rich man and served him without any agreement. Thus he served him a whole year long, and at the end of the year he went to his master and asked him to pay up as much as he thought would be now due. Then the master produced a penny and said, "Here are your wages!" The servant took the coin, went to a rapid brook, and prayed: "Merciful God, how is it that with a whole year's work I have only earned a penny; you, O God, do know whether I deserved but so little. And I will find it out now, and throw this small coin into the water. If it does not sink, I have earned it; but if it sinks, I have not earned it." He then made the sign of the cross, and threw the coin into the brook, but, behold! it sank at once.

Then he bent down, picked out the coin, and gave it back to his master, with the words, "I bring your coin back to you; I have not deserved it. I will serve you another year." And so he began to serve afresh, and when the year had come to an end, again he went to his master and asked him to pay up so much as he thought would be his due. And the master again produced a penny and said, "Here are your wages!" The servant took the coin, thanked his master, and again straightway went to the same rapid brook, made the sign of the cross, threw the money into the water, and said, "Merciful God, if I have justly earned it, let it float on the surface; if not, let the coin sink." But when he threw the coin into the brook, again it sank immediately to the bottom. Then he bent down, picked it out, and once more returning to his master, he said, "Sir, here is your penny back; I have not earned it yet. I will serve you another year." And so he began to serve afresh; and when the third year had come to an end, again he went to his master and asked him to pay him as much as he thought he had earned. The master, however, gave him but a penny, and he took it and thanked him, and went again to the brook to see whether perhaps he had earned it now. When he arrived he made the sign of the cross and threw the penny into the water, praying, "Merciful God, if I have earned this penny, let it float; if not, let it sink!" But this time the penny did not sink; it floated. The joyful servant picked it out, put it into his pocket, and went away with it into a wood. Here he built for himself a tiny cottage, and led a happy and contented life.

After a time he heard that his master was getting ready to set out for a long sea voyage to a country ever so far away. He went to him and asked him to buy him something for his penny on the other side of the sea. The master promised him to do so, took the penny, and started. Whilst he was on the way he met some children near the shore who were about to kill a cat and throw it into the sea. When the master saw this he hurried towards them, and asked them, "What are you doing, children?" They answered him, "This cat is a nuisance, therefore we are going to kill it." Then the master took the penny which his former servant had given him, and offered it to the children for their cat. The children were pleased with the bargain, and gave the cat to the merchant. And he carried the cat on board his ship and continued his voyage. Then arose a violent storm that blew the ship out of her right course, and for three months the travellers did not know where they were. When the storm abated and the master had quite lost his way, he travelled a little farther, and at last he arrived in front of a fortified town. No sooner had the ship arrived than the townspeople, hearing about a ship from strange lands, poured out of the fortress to see her, and one of them, a rich man, invited the ship's master to sup with him.

When the invited guest arrived, lo ! what a sight he beheld ! Everywhere there were rats and mice, and servants armed with sticks stood on all sides to ward off the horrid animals. Then the merchant said to the master of the house, " My dear friend, what is the meaning of all this?" Whereupon his host said, " It is always like this with us; we have no rest from these animals, neither during dinner nor during supper. And when we go to sleep each one of us has a box in which he locks himself up, so that the mice cannot gnaw off his ears."

Then the master of the ship remembered the cat he had bought for a penny, and said to his host, " I have an animal on board my ship that will settle all this in two or three days." The host replied, " My friend, if you will let us have that wonderful animal of yours, and if it will do what you say it can do, we shall fill your ship with silver and gold."

After supper the merchant went to his ship to fetch the cat, and told his host that everybody might go to bed without fear now. But the people had not got the courage, and the merchant was the only one who dared to sleep outside a box. Then he let loose his cat. And she began a most awful slaughter. Mouse after mouse, rat after rat, she killed, until in the morning a high heap of corpses was piled up. Three days later not a single mouse nor a single rat was left. Then the host filled our traveller's ship with gold and silver, and the latter returned home.

When he arrived home his old servant came and asked what he had bought him for his penny. Then the master gave him a square slab of marble, beautifully polished and cut, and said, "See, this beautiful marble I have bought you for your penny." The servant was much pleased, took it home, and made a table out of it. The next day he went out to fetch wood, but when he returned home, behold, the whole of the marble had been changed into gold, and it was shining like the sun, filling the tiny cottage with a dazzling light. The honest servant was frightened, ran to his master, and said, "Master, what have you given me? That gold cannot be mine; come and look at it." The master went, and when he saw what a miracle God had wrought, he said, "There is no getting away from it, my dear friend: him whom the Almighty God is helping, all the Saints will help! Come with me and receive what is yours!" And thereupon he gave to him everything he had brought along in his ship, and, moreover, he gave unto him in marriage his beloved and only daughter.

THE CASTLE IN CLOUDLAND

Once upon a time there lived a Tsar who had three sons and one daughter. The latter he brought up behind lock and key, and he guarded her like the very apple of his eyes. When the maiden grew up she asked her father one evening to allow her to take a little stroll with her brothers, and the Tsar permitted her to do so. But hardly had the four stepped out of the castle gate when a dragon came flying along, seized the princess, and carried her away out of the midst of her brothers up into the clouds. As quickly as they could the brothers hastened to their father and told him what had happened, and said they were quite ready to sally forth in search of their sister. The Tsar approved of their proposal, gave a horse to each of them, and everything else necessary for the expedition; and thus they went away.

After a long journey they sighted a castle that was built neither on the earth nor in the sky, but appeared to hover among the clouds. When they came nearer they considered whether it might not be possible that the young princess had been carried there, and they took counsel together as to how they could get up to her. After much careful reflection and discussion, they decided to kill one of their horses, cut its hide into strips, make thereof a very long thong, fasten an arrow to the extreme end, and shoot it upwards into the castle.

After that, should the arrow stick fast, they would climb up the thong.

The two younger brothers asked the eldest to kill his horse, but he would not do so, and when the second refused likewise, the youngest killed his horse, made a very long thong out of the hide, fixed an arrow to its extreme end, and shot it straight up into the castle. Now one of them would have to climb up; again the two elder brothers refused, and only the youngest was ready to do it. Arrived in the castle above, he began to wander from one room to another, until at last he entered an apartment in which to his great joy he beheld his sister. She was sitting upon a couch, and the dragon had put down his head into her lap and slept. When she beheld her brother, she was very much frightened, and implored him urgently to escape before the dragon should awake. Yet he paid no heed to her words, but seized his club, whirled it around, and gave the dragon a blow on the head. The dragon, however, heavy with sleep, touched the spot with his hand and said to the trembling princess, " Something is biting me here." As soon as he had said that the prince gave him a second blow, but again the dragon only murmured, " Something is biting me here." But when the prince lifted up his arm to strike a third time his sister pointed out to him the only spot where the dragon could be mortally wounded. The moment the club touched the spot the dragon lay dead. The princess threw him down from her lap, leaped up, hastened to embrace and kiss her brother, and thanked him for her deliverance. Then she took him by the hand, in order to show him all the rooms of the castle one after another. At first she led him into a room, in which stood a black steed tied to the manger, and its whole harness was made of pure silver. Next she led him into a second room; there, tied to its manger, stood a white horse that had a harness of pure gold. At last she led him into a third room; there stood by the manger a mouse-coloured horse whose harness was studded with beautiful jewels.

Out of this room she then led him into an apartment in which a maiden was sitting, bending over a golden tambourette and embroidering with golden threads. Out of this room she led him into another, where again a maiden sat spinning golden threads; finally she led him into a room, where a third maiden was threading pearls, and in front of her a golden hen with her chickens was picking up pearls from a golden plate.

After they had been round in this fashion for a time and inspected everything, the princess returned once more to the room where the dragon lay dead, pulled him out of it, and threw the carcase down to the earth. Her brothers below were almost mad with terror, so awful was the sight of the dragon. After that the youngest brother first lowered his sister, then the three maidens one after another, each with her work. And whilst he was thus hard at work he considered whose would be this one or that one, but when it was the third maiden's turn—the maiden who had the golden hen and the chickens—he resolved, " She shall be mine!"

The brothers, however, were envious that he had been such a hero, and had found and delivered their sister. They therefore cut the thong, so that he was unable to come down himself. Then they took a shepherd whom they found with his sheep in the fields, dressed him up so that he looked like the youngest brother, and thus they went home to their father. And the three maidens were strictly forbidden to say anything of the true state of things.

After some time the youngest brother who had had to stay behind in the castle, heard that his brothers and the shepherd were making preparations to marry the maidens he had delivered. On the day when the eldest brother's wedding was to take place he mounted the black steed, and at the moment when the wedding guests were leaving the church he alighted amongst them, gave his brother the bridegroom a gentle blow on the back with his club, so that he fell instantly to the ground, whilst the youngest brother on his black steed flew back to his castle. When he learned that the second brother was about to marry, seated on the white horse he came flying along. When the wedding guests were leaving the church he gently struck the bridegroom's shoulder, so that he at once fell from his horse; and again the youngest brother raced away back to the castle. But when at last the news came that the shepherd was going to marry the maiden he had chosen for his own, he mounted the mouse-coloured horse and came flying along just when the wedding guests were leaving the church, and he struck such a blow on the bridegroom's head that he fell down dead. The wedding guests made a rush to catch him, but he had no desire to escape. He stayed amongst them and revealed to them that he, and not the shepherd, was the Tsar's youngest son. He told them how the two wicked brothers out of envy had deserted him in that castle where he had found his sister and killed her captor. His sister and the three maidens bore witness to the prince's tale. When the Tsar heard this he was so infuriated with his two elder sons that he sent them away into exile. Then he married the youngest son to his chosen bride; and when the old Tsar died in a short time, the youngest prince became his successor, and the new Tsar and his beautiful bride lived happily ever after.

THE WONDERFUL HAIR

Once upon a time there lived a man who was poor. And he had many children whom he could not keep, so that several times he had been on the point of killing them all in order not to see them die of hunger. And it was but due to the pleadings of his wife that he did not do it. Now one night, whilst he was asleep, a lovely child appeared to him and said, " Oh, man, I see you are about to sacrifice the salvation of your soul by killing your poor children. I know you are in great distress, and therefore I have come to help you. To-morrow morning early you shall find under your pillow a mirror, a red handkerchief, and an embroidered scarf. Take these three things, and without telling anyone go into the forest. There you will discover a river; walk along it till you come to its fountain-head, and there you will behold a maiden resplendent as the sun with long hair flowing over her shoulders, but she wears no clothes, just as she was born. But beware, and do not speak a word, unless you want something evil to befall you, for at the first sound you utter she will bewitch you and turn you into a fish or something similar and eat you. If, however, she tells you to scratch her head gently, do not refuse, and then when you rummage through her hair and find one that is as red as blood, pull it out and hasten back with it; and if the maiden should notice it and begin to run after you, then let drop first the embroidered scarf, next the red handkerchief, and finally the mirror. Each time she will tarry a moment, and these delays will help you to escape. Try then to sell the hair to a rich man, and take care not to be defrauded, for the hair is of enormous value; you will be a rich man with the money you can get for it, and you will be able to keep your children."

When the poor man awoke in the morning he actually found everything under his pillow just as the child had told him in his dream. At once he set out and went into the forest. When he had discovered the river, he followed its course till he reached its fountain-head. Looking about there he beheld the maiden, who was sitting on the edge of the spring catching sun-beams, which she drew through a needle in order to embroider a cloth woven from the hair of heroes. As soon as she caught sight of him she rose and said, " Whence do you come, unknown hero?" But he answered nothing. So she asked him again, "Who are you, and why have you come here?" and many other questions. But he remained as dumb as a stone. Only with his hands he made signs that he was dumb, and had come for help. Then she told him that he was to sit down at her feet, and bending down her head, she asked him softly to scratch it. Without hesitation he did so, and eagerly searched for the red hair, and hardly had he found it, than he separated it carefully from the others, plucked it out, leaped up, and ran away with it as fast as his legs would carry him.

The maiden, noticing this, and not less swift than he, rushed after him, and soon was close on his heels, when, turning round, he saw she was fast overtaking him; so he threw down the embroidered scarf as he had been told. When she beheld the scarf she stopped running, and commenced to examine it thoroughly and to admire the embroidery. Meanwhile the man gained again considerably. Then the maiden hid the scarf in her bosom and hastened after him. And when once more he saw himself almost overtaken, he threw down the red handkerchief, over which she tarried, gazing at it in admiration, so that the poor man succeeded in gaining further ground. Angry on perceiving this, the maiden now threw away scarf and handkerchief, and pursued him once more. Now being very much pressed, he threw down the mirror. The maiden had never seen a mirror in her life. So she picked it up, and beholding herself in it, she thought another being similar to herself was gazing at her, and whilst she was lost in the contemplation of it the man covered such a great distance that she would never have been able to overtake him. So she gave up the pursuit and returned home.

The poor man, however, well and cheerful, reached his house, showed the hair to his wife and children, and related all that had happened. His wife laughed and sneered at him on account of that red hair; however, he paid no attention to her, but went into the nearest town to sell the red hair.

Soon a number of curious people gathered around him, several merchants amongst them. One of them offered him a sovereign, another two sovereigns for it. Higher and still higher prices were offered until the bidding had risen to one hundred pounds. By that time the Tsar, too, had heard about it, and he ordered the man to be brought before him, and offered him a thousand pounds for the hair. At this price the man sold it to him. Now, what was the matter with this hair? The Tsar split it carefully into two, and found in it the records of many events worth knowing that had happened since the creation of the world.

Thus the man became rich, and henceforth with his wife and children he lived happily ever after. And the child that had appeared to him in a dream had been an angel sent by our Lord God, who wanted to help the poor man, and also because He chose that in this way the mysterious facts and wonderful deeds recorded within that hair should see the light of day, for these facts and deeds had never until then been revealed.

CLOTHES MADE OF DEW AND SUN-RAYS

Once upon a time there was an emperor, the father of an only daughter, whose beauty was great beyond all belief. The emperor caused an announcement to be made that he would give her in marriage to a youth who could guess what kind of birthmark she had and where it was. In addition the fortunate young man was to have half his empire. But anyone who failed to guess the truth would either be turned into a black lamb or have his head chopped off. The news soon spread throughout the world, and thousands of suitors came, but all in vain. An incredibly large number of youths were turned into black lambs; the others had their heads chopped off.

The rumour about the beautiful princess also reached a youth, who, though poor, was thoughtful and wise. He was seized with a great longing to possess both the maiden and the half share in the empire. So he set out, and went not to woo the girl, but just to see her and ask her something.

When he came to the Imperial Court he beheld most remarkable things. The place simply swarmed with lambs of all kinds, and gambolling about him, they began to bleat as though they wanted to induce him to desist from his plan lest he too might be turned into a black lamb; at the same time all the chopped-off heads stuck on poles in a long row began to shed tears. When he saw this, the horror of it overwhelmed him so that he was just on the point of retracing his steps. But a man clad in a blood-soaked garment, with wings and with only one eye in the middle of his forehead, stopped him and said, "Where are you going? Back, else you are lost!" Then he turned back again and betook himself to the princess, who was already waiting for him, and asked, "Are you, too, come to marry me?" "No, happy princess, but since I have heard that you intend getting married I have come to inquire whether you might not be in need of really beautiful bridal clothes?" "And what kind of garments are they which you could offer me?" she asked; and he replied, "I have ever such pretty hose made of marble; a dainty skirt made of dew; a shawl into which are woven golden sun-rays, the stars, and the moon; I have also wonderful shoes made of purest gold, and they are neither a shoemaker's nor a goldsmith's work. If you desire to buy all these nice things, command me and I will fetch them. But you must know this, if you want to try on these grand garments one after another, no one but myself must be permitted to be present. If the clothes should fit you, I am sure we shall come to terms; if they do not fit you, I undertake not to show them to anybody else, but will keep them for my own future bride." The princess was allured by his description, and ordered him to fetch the things. He went and brought everything, and God only knows how he came by these garments.

Both now locked themselves in a room, and she

began by first putting on the hose. He, however, paid the greatest attention whether he might not behold the mole somewhere, and, lo! fortunately he noticed it near her right knee, and it looked like a golden star. Of course he did not betray that he had seen the mole, and only thought to himself, "Well, I have made my fortune for the remainder of my life." Then the princess tried on the dainty skirt and all the other things, but he paid no longer any heed whether there might be another mark. Everything fitted her as though it had been specially made for her. They then concluded the bargain, and she paid him what he asked. He took his money, and procured for himself the most magnificent and splendid raiments that could be found anywhere. And some days afterwards he went to the emperor to seek the princess in marriage.

When he stepped before the emperor he commenced speaking, "Most gracious emperor! I have come to ask for your daughter's hand; do not refuse her to me!" "Very well," said the emperor to him, "but do you know in what manner men have to woo my daughter? Beware! if you do not guess the mark she has, you are lost; but if you can guess its place, my daughter shall be yours and with her half the empire." Then he bowed to the emperor and said, "Praise be unto you, emperor and father-in-law of mine! If that is so, she belongs to me, for I know she has a golden star on her right knee." The emperor was amazed that he knew this, and since he saw no other way out of it he gave him his daughter in marriage, and the wedding was duly celebrated.

When the question arose of sharing the empire with him, the son-in-law said, "Willingly I shall renounce half of your empire if you will give back their true shape to these unfortunate men who either have been turned into lambs or had their heads chopped off." Then the emperor said, "To do that is not within my power; only my daughter can restore their true form to these men." Then he appealed to his daughter, and she said, "Very well, let the physicians bleed me underneath this star on my knee. Let every lamb lick up a little of the blood which will well forth, and let the lower lip of each head upon the poles be touched with it, and at once the lambs will resume their natural human shape and the heads will be restored to life and become human beings as before.

This was accordingly done, and when all had resumed their original shape the bridegroom invited them all to be his guests at the wedding; and with much singing and beating of drums he took the maiden home. After he had entertained his guests there too with food and drink, everybody went to his own home, but his newly-wedded wife stayed with him. And God knows what else befell them after this, of which nowadays one no longer troubles to think.

FATE

Once upon a time there were two brothers who lived together in a house; the one did all the work, whereas the other one went about idling and never did anything but eat and drink. And they had abundance of everything, and were blessed with cattle, horses, sheep, pigs, and bees.

Then the brother who did all the work one day said to himself," "Why should I work for that lazy bones as well? It is much better we separate; I shall work for myself and he may do what he likes." And so he told his brother, "It is not fair that I have to manage everything whilst you never lend me a hand. You think of nothing but eating and drinking. I have, therefore, made up my mind. We are going to part." The brother, however, tried to dissuade him and said, "You have the management of everything, both of your property and of mine. And you know I am quite content and agree with everything you do." But the industrious brother insisted, so that the other one had to give in, and he said, "Very well, I shall not be cross with you about it; go and give me my share according to what you think is mine." Then everything was divided up. The lazy brother took his share, and at once he appointed a cow-keeper for his cattle, a stable-boy for his horses, a goatherd, a swine-herd, and a bee-keeper, and he said to them, "All my property I leave in your hands and God's." And after that he stayed at home, unconcerned, and without troubling himself about anything. The other brother went on working hard as before, looked after his herds, and was most careful. Yet in spite of that he did not thrive, but suffered many losses, and his affairs became daily worse and worse. At last he was so poor that he had not even a pair of latchet shoes, and had to walk about barefooted. Then he said to

I

himself, " I will go to my brother to see how he is getting on."

His way led him past a meadow, in which there was a flock of sheep, and when he came nearer he saw there was no shepherd, but an exceedingly beautiful maiden who was spinning a golden thread. After he had greeted the girl with a friendly " God be with you," he asked her whose were those sheep. She replied, " To whom I belong, his are also the sheep." Then he asked her, " Who are you?" whereupon she answered, " I am your brother's Good Luck." Then overcome with violent anger, he asked, " Where is my Good Luck?" The maiden said, " Oh, that is very far from you." " And could I find it?" he asked. " You may," she said; " go and search for it." And when he had heard this and seen that his brother's sheep were so fine that one cannot possibly imagine any sheep more valuable, then he was no longer inclined to view the other herds, but he went straightway to his brother. When the latter beheld him he pitied him, and with tears in his eyes he said, " Where have you been all this time?" And noticing the poor garments and bare feet, he gave him a pair of latchet shoes and some money. After he had been entertained for a few days the poor brother started again for home. Arrived there, he took a knapsack over his shoulders, put some bread in it, took a staff in his hands, and went into the wide world to find his Good Luck.

When he had been walking for some time, he came into a big forest, and there he found an ugly trollop sleeping underneath a shrub. Then he lifted his stick and struck her on the back to awaken her. She got up with difficulty, could hardly open her bleared eyes, and said, "You may thank God that I had fallen asleep here, for had I been awake you would not have received those lovely shoes." Then he asked her, "Who are you that on your account I should not have been given these shoes?" The slut said, "I am your Good Luck." When he heard this he grew very angry, saying, "So you are my Good Luck? I wish God would kill you. Who is it that has given you unto me?" The slut, however, interrupted him, "Fate has given me unto you." Then he asked, "Where is this Fate?" And she said, "Go and search for it!" with which words she disappeared.

Thereupon the man started again on his way in order to find Fate. And whilst he was thus going along he came to a village, and there stood a fine house in which a large fire was burning. Then he thought to himself, "Here must be a wedding, or they are celebrating some other feast-day!" He entered, and saw hanging over the fire a big kettle in which the supper was cooking, and the master of the house sat by the fire. He wished him a good evening, to which the master of the house replied, "May God bestow on you all good things!" invited him to take a seat near him, and asked him who he was and whither he was going. Then he told everything, how he, too, had been a householder, how he had become poor, and that he was now on his way to ask Fate herself why just he himself should remain so poor. Hereupon he asked the master of the house why and for whom he was cooking such a big meal. Then the latter said, "Alas! my brother! I am the master of a house and have abundance of everything, but nevertheless I am unable to appease the hunger of my people; it is as though dragons were hidden in their stomachs. Just observe my people when we are going to supper, then you will see it." And when they sat down for supper the men snatched and grabbed one another's food, and in a few minutes the large cauldron was empty. After supper the host's young wife collected all the bones and threw them on a heap behind the stove. And when the stranger was wondering at this, suddenly two very old persons thin as skeletons crawled forth in order to suck the bones. Then the stranger asked the master of the house, "Who are those behind the stove?" And he answered, "They are my father and my mother, and they will not die, just as though they were chained to this world."

The next morning when they parted the stranger was requested kindly to ask Fate why the people in his house could not be sufficiently fed, and why his father and mother were so long in dying. The visitor promised to do so, and took his leave in order to find Fate.

After he had been on the road for ever such a long time, one evening he came into another village, entered one of the houses, and asked for a night's shelter. Readily he was received, and when asked what was his destination, he told them everything. Then the people in the house said, "For God's sake, brother, when you have reached your goal, do ask why our cattle do not thrive but are getting thinner and thinner." He promised to ask Fate about it, and the next morning he set out again.

And he came to a river and called out, "Oh, water, water, carry me over to the other bank;" The water asked him, "Where are you going?" And he told the water. Then the water carried him across and said, "Please, brother, ask Fate why nothing can live within me." And he promised to do the water this favour and went on.

After ever such a long time at last he came into a forest, and here he met a hermit, whom he asked whether he could give him any information about Fate. And the hermit said to him, "Go from here straight across the mountains, then you will arrive exactly in front of Fate's castle. But there you must not say a word, only do all the time precisely the same thing Fate is doing until she puts questions to you." The man thanked the hermit, and set out on his journey across the mountains. When he arrived at the castle of Fate, what things he did behold! Everywhere imperial splendour, and a great number of servants, men and women, were running about. But Fate sat quite alone at a table eating her supper. When the man saw her for whom he had been searching such a long time, he sat down by her side and shared the supper. After supper Fate lay down to rest. So did he. Toward midnight there was the most awful noise and turmoil in the castle, but above all the turmoil a voice was audible that said, "O Fate! O Fate! One hundred thousand souls have been born to-day. Give them something according to your pleasure!"

Then Fate rose, opened a treasure-box full of gold, took out of it glittering sovereigns, and scattered them all over the floor of the room. At the same time she said, " As I am faring to-day, they shall fare all their lives."

At day-break the magnificent castle was gone, and in its place stood quite a small house of modest appearance. Yet there was in it enough and to spare of everything. When evening fell, Fate again sat down to supper; so did our friend, and neither spoke a word. And after supper both lay down to rest. Towards midnight there was again the most awful noise and turmoil, and above all the turmoil a voice was again audible that said, " O Fate! O Fate! One hundred thousand souls have been born to-day. Give them something according to your pleasure!" Then Fate rose, opened a money box, but there were no sovereigns, only silver coins with an occasional sovereign hidden away amongst them, and Fate scattered silver coins all over the floor of the room. At the same time she said, " As I am faring to-day they shall fare all their lives."

And at day-break that small but comfortable house was gone too, and in its place stood one ever so much smaller. So it happened every night and every morning the house was smaller, until at last there remained but a wretched hut, and Fate took a spade and began digging. Then the man, our friend, likewise took a spade and began digging, and both kept on digging throughout the day. When evening fell, Fate took a piece of bread, halved it, and gave one-half to the man. That was their supper, and when they had eaten it they lay down to rest. Toward midnight there was again the most awful noise and turmoil, and above all the turmoil a voice was yet again audible that said, "O Fate! O Fate! One hundred thousand souls have been born to-day. Give them something according to your pleasure!" Then Fate rose, opened a box, and began scattering about small potsherds like those with which children play, and amongst them a very few coins. At the same time she said, "As I am faring to-day they shall fare all their lives."

But when day broke again the hut had once more been changed into a large palace, just as grand as the one which the man found when he arrived. And now at last Fate spoke to him and asked him, "Why did you come here?" And then he related all the particulars of his distress and his troubles, and that he had come to ask Fate personally why she had given unto him such a Bad Luck. Then Fate said to him, "You have seen how during the first night I was scattering sovereigns, and you have noticed, I hope, everything that happened during that night. Exactly as I am faring during the night in the course of which a man is born, thus he will fare throughout his life. You have been born in a night of poverty, and therefore you will remain poor as long as you live. Your brother, on the other hand, has seen the light of the world during a fortunate night, and he will be a fortunate man until the end of his days. But since you have taken so much trouble and come in quest of me, I will tell you how you can help yourself. Your brother has a daughter; her name is Milica, and she is just as fortunate as her father. When you get home again, take her to you into your house, and of everything that you may gain say, " It is Milica's !"

Then he thanked Fate and said, " I know of a rich farmer who has more than enough of everything, yet he never succeeds in feeding his household well; at every meal they empty a brewer's copper full of food, and even that is not enough for them. And the father and the mother of this farmer, as though they were chained to this earth, have grown quite black with age and they are shrivelled up like ghosts; yet they cannot die. Therefore he begged me when I was his guest for a night to ask you what is the reason of all that." Then Fate replied, " All that happens because he does not honour his father and mother, and just throws some food at them behind the stove. If he would put them in the place of honour at his table and hand to them the first glass of wine and the first glass of whisky, they would soon breathe their last, and the people of the farmer's household would no longer eat so much."

Then he asked Fate, " In another village where I was staying a night a man complained to me that his cattle would not thrive, and he urged me to find out from you whose fault it is." And Fate said, " It is because on the day of the patron saint of his house he slaughters the most wretched cow he has; if, on the other hand, he would kill the very best, all his cattle would thrive."

Finally, he also inquired on behalf of the water, "And how is it that nothing can live in that water?" And Fate answered, " Because no human being has yet been drowned in it. But take heed not to tell the water about this secret before you have been carried across lest the water should at once drown you!"

Once again he thanked Fate, and started on his journey home. When he came to the water, it asked, "Well, what did Fate say?" and he answered, "First carry me across, and then I will tell you." Hardly had the water carried him across than he began running, and when he was a good distance away he turned round and called out, "O, Water, it is because you have never drowned a human being that nothing will live in you." On hearing this, the water rushed after him over the fields and meadows, and only with great difficulty he escaped.

When he came into the village to the man whose cattle were not thriving, he was already impatiently awaited. "What news do you bring me, brother? Have you questioned Fate?" Whereupon he replied, "Yes, I have done so—and Fate said it is because you always offer up the worst cow on the feast-day of your household saint; but if you would sacrifice your best, all your cattle would thrive." Having heard this, the farmer said, "Brother, stay with us! There are but three days to the feast of our patron saint, and if that is true which you tell me, I'll show you my gratitude." When now the feast-day came, the father of the family killed the finest bullock which he had, and from that moment onwards his cattle began to thrive. Then he gave the man five oxen as a present. And the man set out again.

And when he arrived in the village where the ever-hungry household was, he was greeted with the words, "For God's sake, tell me, brother, how are you and what did Fate say?" And he replied, "Fate says you are not honouring your father and your mother, and you always throw the food at them behind the stove. If you would put them at the table, and, moreover, in the place of honour at the top of the table, hand them the first glass of wine and the first glass of whisky, the inmates of your house would not eat half as much, and your father and mother would depart this life." When the master of the house had heard this, he told his wife at once to wash and to comb her father and mother-in-law and to dress them nicely. When the evening came the two were placed at the top of the table and the first glass of wine and the first glass of whisky were handed to them. From that moment onwards the inmates of that household could no longer eat so much, and the father and mother in a few days died peaceably. Then the grateful master of the house gave our friend two bullocks, and the latter, after thanking his host, went home.

When he came into his native place his acquaintances met him and asked him, "Whose are these beautiful cattle?" and he said each time, "My friend, they belong to Milica, my brother's daughter." When he arrived home, he went at once to his brother and begged him, "Do give me Milica, brother, as you know I have no one to care for me." And his brother replied, "I do not mind at all, go and take Milica with you." Then he led his brother's daughter to his house. From that moment onwards he prospered much, but of everything gained he said, " It is Milica's."

One day he went out over his fields to see how the corn was going on. It was most lovely to look at. Then a wanderer came along, who asked him, " Whose is this corn field?" And forgetting himself for a moment, he said, " It's mine." In the moment he said that flames burst out of the corn and the fire spread rapidly. Quickly he ran after the wanderer and exclaimed, " Stop, my friend, the corn does not belong to me at all; it is Milica's." At once the fire ceased. Henceforth he lived happily with Milica, and to the end of his days all he did prospered.

SOLOMON CURSED BY HIS MOTHER

Once upon a time the very wise Solomon in a conversation with his mother said that every woman on earth at the bottom of her heart was thoroughly bad. His mother scolded him very much, and said it was not true; and when he proved in some fashion that she, too, was like other women, she grew infuriated and cursed him, and said he was not to die until he had seen the depths of the sea and the heights of heaven.

When Solomon had reached a very great age, and became tired of life and this world, he bethought himself how he could break the spell of his mother's curse so that he might die. First of all he wrought a big iron box, big enough to allow him to sit inside. To the lid of the box he fastened an iron chain, long enough in his opinion to reach the bottom of the sea. Then he climbed into the box, asked his wife to lock it, and to throw it into the sea; but to keep in her hands the end of the chain so that she might be able to pull it up again after the box and the chain had reached the bottom of the sea. Solomon's wife put the lid on, locked the box, and threw it into the sea. Whilst she was now holding in her hands the end of the chain, someone came and deceived her by telling her that the wise Solomon, together with his box, had been swallowed by a great fish already ever such a long time ago, and that she could do no better than let the chain drop and go home. She did so, and the heavy chain pressed the box with the wise Solomon inside firmly on to the bottom of the sea.

Some time after this event the devils found the staff, cap, and stole of St. Johannes, and started a quarrel amongst themselves when dividing these things. At last they agreed to go to the wise Solomon, and he was to settle their differences. When they came to him at the bottom of the sea and told him what they wanted him to do, he said, " How can I decide your case here from within the box where I cannot see either you or the object of your disputes? Carry me up to the surface and put me on the shore, and I will be your umpire." At once the devils carried him up in his box. As soon as the wise Solomon had got out he took into his hands the things about which the devils were quarrelling just as if he was going to examine them and see what they were worth. All of a sudden he made the sign of the cross with the staff of the saint, and then the devils fled, so that all the things became his.

In this way the wise Solomon had beheld the bottom of the sea. Now he bethought himself how he might get a sight of the heights of heaven. For this purpose he caught two ostriches, starved them for a few days, and then he tied to their feet a big basket. Then he sat down in that basket, and in his hands he held on a long spit a roasted lamb just above the heads of the ostriches. Eager to seize the roasted lamb, up flew the ostriches, up and up, and they never stopped till the wise Solomon touched with his spit the vault of heaven. Then he turned his spit downwards, and thus the ostriches carried him again down to earth. And now that he had seen the depths of the sea and the heights of heaven he could die at last.

THE TRIUMPH OF JUSTICE

Once upon a time there was a king who had two sons. The elder was cunning and unjust; the other, however, was good and just to all men. After their father had died, the unjust son said to his brother, " We can no longer live here together. Here are three hundred golden coins and a horse; that is your share in our inheritance, and you must not hope for more." The younger brother took the three hundred golden coins and the horse and started on his way, saying to himself, " God be praised! How large is my share of the whole kingdom!"

After some time the brothers met one another,

and the just one at once greeted his unjust brother, "God be with you, my brother!" The latter, however, returned, "God damn you! Why do you always keep God on your tongue? Injustice is mightier than Justice, whatever you say!" Then the good brother replied, "Very well, let us make a wager that Injustice is not better than Justice." And they wagered for a hundred pounds, and agreed the question should be decided by the first person they would meet.

And whilst they went on their way they met the devil, who had disguised himself as a monk, and they asked him, "What is better, Justice or Injustice?" The devil said, "Injustice!" and the good brother lost one hundred sovereigns. After that they wagered the second hundred, and even the third, and thus, according to the decision of the devil whom they encountered each time, but in a different disguise, the good brother lost all his three hundred golden coins. And after that he wagered and lost his horse. But he said, "God be praised! Though I have no longer any sovereigns, I have still my eyes, and now I will even wager with these." And thus he bet with his eyes that Justice was a finer thing than Injustice. But the bad brother, no longer troubling about an umpire, took a knife and cut out his brother's eyes, saying, "Now that you are without eyes, let Justice help you." The pitiable blind brother, however, praised God and said, "I have given away my eyes for the sake of God's justice; now I ask you, my brother, kindly to give me just some water in a basin that I may moisten my lips and wash my wounds, and then lead me forth and leave me beneath the fir-tree by the spring." The brother complied, gave him some water, led him forth, and left him beneath the fir-tree by the spring.

While the unfortunate youth was thus sitting there, all at once during the night he heard how the Vile came to the spring and bathed therein. And he heard one say to another, " Do you know, sisters, the king's daughter lies stricken with leprosy. The king has called together all his physicians, but not one is able to cure her. Of course, if anyone of them but knew it, this water here taken immediately after our visit and prepared as a bath for the princess would cure her within twenty-four hours, just as anybody dumb, blind, or lame can be healed by it!" Then the cock began to crow, and the Vile disappeared. The poor wretched man now dragged himself, crawling on his hands and feet, from the fir-tree to the water, washed his eyes with it, and, lo! his sight was immediately restored.

Thereupon he filled the basin with this water, hastened to the king whose daughter was ill with leprosy, and said to him, " I have come to heal your daughter; if she will admit me she shall be cured within twenty-four hours." And as soon as the king had heard this, he admitted him at once into the maiden's apartment, and gave the order that she was to be bathed in this water. Thereafter, when one day and one night had passed by, the maiden was well again and quite clean from leprosy. The king, highly delighted, gave the youth half the kingdom and his daughter as his wife, and thus he became the king's son-in-law and the first in the land after the king.

The tidings of all this soon spread throughout the whole kingdom and soon his brother heard about it too, the wicked brother who had said that Injustice was better than Justice. He thought, "My brother must have found his Good Luck under the fir-tree." So he went there himself to find his. First he took some water in a basin, then he sat underneath the fir-tree, took a knife, and cut out his eyes. When night had fallen at the same hour the Vile returned to have another bathe and they discussed how the king's daughter had been healed, and they said, "Someone must have listened to us when we said that she could be healed through this water. Perhaps he is even listening now; come, let us see!" And in their searching they came to the fir-tree, discovered him who had come to find his Good Luck, him who had always said that Injustice is better than Justice. They seized him and tore him into four pieces. Thus did Injustice deal with that accursed man.

PROVERBS

"They show with what a treasure of worldly wisdom and sensible views the Serbian people are endowed."

J. GRIMM

PROVERBS

A cheese that weeps and a whisky that warms are worth something.
A dog that is to be killed is named a mad dog.
A girl finds a husband on account of her face.
A good reputation is known far and wide, but a bad reputation reaches even to the ends of the earth.
A honeyed mouth opens iron gates.
A man may show to his friends his wife, his weapons, and his horse; but he should never entrust either to their hands.
A mighty river owes its power to the little brooks.
An apple that ripens late keeps longest.
A sheep which finds its own wool burdensome is, like its wool, worth nothing.
As long as a man does not dishonour himself, nobody else can.
As long as a man is begging he has a golden mouth; but he turns nasty when he is to repay.
A stupid fox traps himself with one foot but a clever one with all four.
A sulking priest will get no stipend.
Avoid both the fool and the saint !
Barking dogs do not trouble the sea.
Beat a bad man and he will but grow worse.
Better to be in the grave than to live a slave.
Better to be the cock for one day than the hen for a month.
Blame a man when he can hear you; praise him when he is away.

Boast when you are with strangers, but complain only to your own people.
Even God has not been able to please everybody.
Even our favourite guest is a bore after three days.
Even the cow defends herself with her tail.
Even the holy Patriarch when hungry will steal a piece of bread.
Every one attempts to bring all the water he can to his own mill.
Every parson's purse is deep.
Fortune at first gives you a glass brimming over with blossoms; woo her again and she hands you a glass full of wine; marry a third wife and the glass is filled with poison.
Give me a friend who will weep with me; those who will laugh with me I can find myself.
God comes with velvet feet, but with hands of iron.
God does not love a man who never suffered.
God is with the worker.
He is not an honest man who has burnt his tongue and does not tell the company that the soup is hot.
He who buys what he does not want will soon have to sell the things he does want.
He who deceives me once is a scoundrel, but he who deceives me often is a smart man.
He who has not learnt something at twenty years of age, nor saved something at thirty, will be a burden to his family.
He who mixes with the refuse ought not to be astonished if the pigs devour him.
He who preserves a wise silence speaks well.
He who spares the guilty harms the innocent.

If an old dog barks look out for mischief.
If close enough even a green branch will be burnt together with a dry one.
If Fortune does not wait for you you cannot overtake her even with the fastest horse.
If one has not got the penny, a palace is too dear even at that price.
If you do not feed the cat you must feed the mice.
If you want to know what is in a man, place him in authority.
It is an easy job to shoot from behind a big tree.
It is an easy matter to throw a stone into the Danube, but very difficult to get it out again.
It is better to die than to have evil offspring.
It is better to return in the middle of one's journey than to pursue it to the end on a bad road.
It is the foolish that fight the battle and the wise that drink the wine.
Look at the mother first and then marry her daughter.
Man goes through the world like a bee through the blossoms.
Man is a learner all his life and yet he dies in ignorance.
Man is harder than a rock and more fragile than an egg.
Man resembles an inflated tube.*
Marry with your ears and not with your eyes.†

---

* cf. : "heu, eheu ! utres inflati ambulamus." (Seleucus in Petronii Cena Trimalchionis.)

† cf. : Nietzsche ; Human, All-Too-Human : " Before entering on a marriage one should ask one's self the question, ' Do you think you will pass your time well with

Meat is only good when outside the hide and fish when out of the water.
Mightier than the Tsar's will is the will of God.
My castle may be small but I am the governor.
My head will suffice to pay even for the Tsar's.
No grass is left where an army passes.
Not the thought is the sin, but the deed.
One should cease praying to a saint who does not help.
People always chastise the fiddler of truth with his own bow.
People with white hands like other people's work best.
Pigs do not bite one another, but as soon as they behold the wolf they fight him, united.
Priest *and* peasant know more than the priest alone.
Poverty and a cough cannot be concealed.
Rather fight with a hero than kiss a coward.
Scarcely has the hungry beggar-woman eaten her fill than she wants people to call her Madam.
Since we cannot do as we will, we will do as we can.
Some people can even make lead float where others will see their very straws sink.
Sooner will a mother forget her off-spring than God his creatures.
Speak the truth but then clear out quickly.
Strike out new roads but stick to your old friends.

this woman till your old age?' All else in marriage is transitory; talk, however, occupies most of the time of the association." Of course the transitoriness of beauty and the great importance of sound information about character and affairs of the " intended " are stressed by the Serbian proverb.

PROVERBS

The coals under the slack burn you most.
The edge of a woman's tongue is keener than that of a Turkish sword.
The estimate of travelling expenditure is no good on the journey.
The grave-digger buries exactly what the cradle lulled to sleep.
The man who has no sense of honour is without a soul.
The man who says right is right will never possess even a cow to milk.
The man who weeps over the world will die without eyes.
The merchant is a huntsman.*
The ox is tied by his horns, man by his tongue.
There is as little measure in the Main as faithfulness in fickle men.
There is no need to pray for rain and death.
There is no stronghold more impregnable than a poor man.†
The soldier in peace time is to us what the stove is in summer.
The wind blows strongest when it is just about to drop.
Three hundred good intentions in the evening; in the morning : but Hell's paving-stones.
To run away is disgraceful but decidedly useful.
Trust no one but yourself and your steed.
Twice only man rejoices, when he marries a wife and when he buries her.

* cf. : " Who but a fool would have faith in a tradesman's ware or his word."—*Tennyson.*
† Because he has nothing and fears nothing.

Vineyards have no need of prayers but of mattocks.
What the winter wears out the summer does not see.
When the thunder roars loudest the rain is nothing.
Where big bells clang the small ones cannot be heard.
Where the devil cannot do anything he sends an old woman to work for him.
Who possesses the shore possesses the sea; and the castle is his who holds the plain.
Why is the devil so wise? Because he is so old.
Woe to the mother-in-law who has to live in the house of her son-in-law.
You cannot possibly bake ginger-bread for all the world.
You must not bark if you cannot bite!

BIBLIOGRAPHY

BIBLIOGRAPHY.

Yovanovitch, V. M.—*An English Bibliography On The Near Eastern Question* (1481-1906). 1909; Belgrade. pp. 111.
Novaković, S.—*Srpska biblijografija za noviju književnost*. 1869; Belgrade. pp. xxiv.+644.
Popović, P.—*Pregled Srpske Književnosti*. 1913; Belgrade. p. 263-362.
Gjorgjević, T. R.—*Zur Einführung in die Serbische Folklore*. 1902; Vienna. pp. 36.
Ćurčin, M.—*Das serbische Volkslied in der deutschen Literatur*. 1905; Leipsic. p. 201-220.

Anonymous.—*Servian Popular Poetry* (Review of Bowring's version). 1827; "The London Magazine," Jan.-April. p. 567-583.
d'Avril, A.—*La Bataille de Kosovo*. 1866; Paris. pp. 65.
Bowring, J.—*Serbian Popular Poetry*. 1827.
Chirol, V.—*Serbia and the Serbs*. 1914; Oxford Pamphlets. pp. 18.
Church, L. F.—*The Story of Servia*. 1914; London. pp. 136.
Ćurčin, M.—*Das serbische Volkslied in der deutschen Literatur*. 1905; Leipsic. pp. 220.
Denton, W. (ed.)—*Serbian Folk-Lore*. (Selected and translated by Madam E. Mijatovies.) 1874; London. pp. vi.+316.
Dozon, A.—*L'Épopée Serbe*. 1888; Paris. pp. lxxx.+335.
Durham, M. A.—*Through the Lands of the Serb*. 1904; London. pp. xi.+345.

Frankl, L. A.—*Gusle Serbische Nationallieder.* 1852; Wien. pp. xxiv.+127.
Gerhard, W.—*Gesänge der Serben.* 1877; Leipzig. pp. 292. (2nd ed.)
Gœthe, W. v.—*Serbische Lieder in "Kunst und Altertum."* 1825. Vol. v., 2; pp. 35-63. *cf.* also v., 1; pp. 84-92; and v., 3; p. 190; and vi., 1; pp. 188-193; and vi., 2; pp. 321-329.
Goetze, P. v.—*Serbische Volkslieder.* 1827; St. Petersburg. pp. vi.+227.
"Göttingische Gelehrte Anzeigen."—*Wuk's Serbische Volksliedersammlung.* 1823; Göttingen. Third volume, pp.1761-1773.
"Göttingische Gelehrte Anzeigen." *Wuk's Serbische Volksliedersammlung.* 1824; Göttingen. Second volume, pp. 809-820.
Jugoslav Committee in London:—The Southern Slav Library. 1915-1916; London. *The Southern Slav Programme;* pp. 32. *The Southern Slavs: Land and People;* pp. 64. *A Sketch of Southern Slav History;* pp. 32. *Southern Slav Culture;* pp. 24.
Kanitz, F.—*Das Königreich Serbien und das Serbenvolk.* 1904-1914; Leipsic. Vol. i., pp. viii.+653; Vol. ii., pp. viii.+595; Vol. iii., pp. viii.+950.
Kapper, S.—*Die Gesänge der Serben.* 1852; Leipzig. Erster Teil : pp. xl.+276. Zweiter Teil : pp. x.+406.
Karadžić, V. S.—*Mala prostonarodna slavenoserbska pesnarica.* Vol. i., pp. 122. Vienna; 1814. Vol. ii., pp. viii.+262. Vienna; 1815.

BIBLIOGRAPHY 157

Karadžić, V. S.—*Narodne Srpske Pjesme.* Vol. i., pp. lxii. + 316. Leipsic; 1824. Vol. ii., p. 305. Leipsic; 1823. Vol. iii., pp. ii. + 399. Leipsic; 1823. Vol. iv., pp. xliv. + 368. Vienna; 1833.
,, *Narodne srpske poslovice, etc.* 1836; Cetinje. pp. l. + 362.
,, *Srpske Narodne Pjesme.* Vienna. Vol. i., pp. xviii. + 640 (1841); Vol. ii., pp. iv. + 664 (1845); Vol. iii., pp. iii. + 592 (1846); Vol. iv., pp. xiv. + 545 (1862); Vol. v., pp. ii. + 559 (1865).
,, *Srpske narodne poslovice, etc.* 1849; Vienna. pp. liii. + 388.
,, *Srpske narodne pripovijetke.* 1853; Vienna. pp. xii. + 263.
,, *Volksmärchen der Serben.* 1854; Berlin (translated into German by Karajich's daughter Wilhelmine, and prefaced by J. Grimm). pp. xii. + 345.
,, *Srpske narodne pripavijetke.* 1870; Vienna. pp. x. + 352.
,, *Srpske Narodne Pjesme.* Belgrade. Vol. i., pp. lxxx. + 662 (1891); Vol. ii., pp. vi. + 648 (1895); Vol. iii., pp. viii. + 552 (1894); Vol. iv., pp. xlvi. + 512 (1896); Vol. v., pp. xxii. + 632 (1898); Vol. vi., pp. xvi. + 577 (1899); Vol. vii., pp. ix. + 504 (1900); Vol. viii., pp. xi. + 579 (1900); Vol. ix., pp. vii. + 603 (1902).

Knolles, R.—*The Generall Historie of the Turks.* 1621; London. (Folio.)

Krauss, F. S.—*Slavische Volksforschungen.* 1908; Leipsic. pp. vii. + 433.

,, *Tausend Sagen u. Märchen der Südslaven.* 1914, etc. Leipsic. pp. xxxiii. + 448.

Kuhać, F. S.—*Južno-Slovjenske Narodne Popievke.* Four vols. 1878-1881. Vol. i., pp. 325; Vol. ii., pp. 305; Vol. iii., pp. 414; Vol. iv., pp. 444.

Lazarović-Hrebelianović, Prince.—*The Servian People.* 1911; London. Two vols. cf., Vol. i., pp. 368-405.

Leger, L.—*Serbes, Croates et Bulgares.* 1913; Paris. pp. 41-52.

Lucerna, C.—*Die südslavische Ballade von Asan Agas Gattin und ihre Nachbildung durch Gœthe.* 1905; Berlin. pp. iv. + 70.

Manojlović, S.—*Serbisch-Croatische Dichtungen.* 1888; Vienna. pp. viii. + 300.

Meredith, Owen (The Earl of Lytton).—*Serbski Pesme.* 1861; London. pp. xxvi. + 142.

,, *The National Songs of Servia.* 1877; Boston. pp. 111.

Mijatović, E. L.—*Kossovo.* 1881; London. pp. vi. + 148.

Mijatović, Č.—*Servia of the Servians.* 1911; London. pp. 98-135; pp. 146-170; pp. 192-221.

Miklosić.—*Über Gœthe's Klagegesang von der edlen Frauen des Asan Aga.* 1883; Vienna. Sitzungsbericht der K. K. Ak. phil.-hist. Kl. 103 vol. 2 Heft. p. 418.

Petrović, V. M.—*Hero Tales and Legends of the Serbians.* 1914; London. pp. xxiii. + 394.

Popović, B., and Popović, P. (editors).—*Srpski Književni Glasnik.* 1901, etc.; Belgrade.

Pypin, A. N., and Spasavić, V. D.—*Geschichte der Slavischen Literaturen.* Vol. i., pp. x.+586 (1880); Vol. ii., pp. xxv.+509 (1883).

" Quarterly Review, The."—*Translations from the Servian Minstrelsy.* 1826; London. (In volume xxxv., pp. 66-81.)

Seton-Watson, R. W.—*The Spirit of the Serb.* 1915; London. pp. 31.

Stead, A. (ed.).—*Servia by the Servians.* 1909; London. pp. 320-336. ("Literature" by P. Popovitch.)

Talvj (Theresa v. Jacob).—*Volkslieder der Serben.* 2nd ed. 1835; Halle and Leipsic. Vol. i., pp. xlvi.+293; Vol. ii., pp. xviii.+330.

,, *Volkslieder der Serben.* New and revised edition. 1853; Leipsic. Vol. i., pp. 1.+310; Vol. ii., pp. 391.

Vogl, J. N.—*Marko Kraljevits.* 1851; Vienna. pp. x.+208.

Voïart, E.—*Chants populaires des Serviens.* 1834; Paris. Vol. i., pp. 308; Vol. ii., pp. 280. (Based on Talvj's version.)

Wesely, E. E.—*Serbische Hochzeitslieder.* 1826; Pest. pp. 97.

" Westminster Review, The."—*Review of Karajich's Collection of Servian Popular Songs.* 1826; May-July. (In Volume vi., pp. 23-39.)

Wratislaw, A. H.—*Sixty Folk-Tales.* 1889; London. pp. xii.+315.

APPENDIX

SERBIAN TEXTS AND MELODIES

JEDNO DRAGO I TO NA DALEKO

("The Absent Lover." See page 47.)

Tavna noći, puna ti si mraka!
Srdce moje još punije jada.
Jad jadujem, nikom ne kazujem:
Majke nemam, da joj jade kažem,
Ni sestrice, da joj se potužim;
Jedno drago, i to na daleko:
Dokle dodje, pola noći prodje,
Dok probuti, p'jevci zapjevaju,
Dok poljubi, saba zora bude:
"Saba zora, ajde, drage, doma."

JEDNO DRAGO I TO NA DALEKO

(Kuhać, Vol. I., Nr. 55.)

BLAGOSOV

("The Lover's Blessing." See page 54.)

Svu noć mi soko prepjeva
    "Ići joj ne ću na svadbu,
Na Milanovu pendžeru:
    "Nego joj šaljem blagosov:
"Ustani gore, Milane!
    "Muškoga ćeda nemala!
"Djevojka ti se udaje,
    "Koliko ljeba pojela,
"I tebe zove na svadbu;
    "Toliko jeda imala!
"Ako joj ne ćeš na svadbu,
    "Koliko vode popila,
"A ti joj pošlji blagosov."—
    "Toliko suza prolila!"
Neka je, nek se udaje!

APPENDIX

BLAGOSOV

(Kuhać, Vol. I., Nr. 82.)

NESREĆNA DEVOJKA

("The Unhappy Bride." See page 49.)

Devojka junaku prsten povraćala:
"Naj ti prsten, momće, moj te rod ne ljubi,
"Ni otac, ni majka, ni brat, ni sestrica;
"Al' me nemoj, momće, na glas iznositi,
"Jer sam ja sirota nesretna devojka:
"Ja bosiljak sejem, meni pelen niće:
"Oj pelen, pelenće, moje gorko cveće!
"Tobom će se moji svati nakititi,
"Kad me stann tužam do groba nositi."

APPENDIX

NESREĆNA DEVOJKA

(*Kuhać, Vol. II., Nr. 711.*)

www.ingramcontent.com/pod-product-compliance
Ingram Content Group UK Ltd.
Pitfield, Milton Keynes, MK11 3LW, UK
UKHW010836280525
6111UKWH00013B/370